THE
GOOD
LIFE

FINDING JOY, PEACE, AND SIMPLICITY IN A
STRESSED-OUT WORLD

BY KAREN AND KEN GONYER

SMITH
FREEMAN
Publishing

The Good Life—Finding Joy, Peace, and Simplicity in a Stressed-Out World

©2019 Smith Freeman Publishing

Bible verses were taken from the following translations:

Cover design by Kim Russell | Wahoo Designs

ISBN: 978-1-7337417-4-3

CONTENTS

THE
GOOD
LIFE

FINDING JOY, PEACE, AND SIMPLICITY IN A
STRESSED-OUT WORLD

KAREN AND KEN GONYER

HOW WE CAME TO WRITE THIS BOOK

I have come that they may have life,
and that they may have it more abundantly.

John 10:10 NKJV

Perhaps you've been thinking about the good life for many years. We certainly have. We've worked together, dreamed together, prayed together, and raised our family together. And as time has passed, and our children have grown up, we've watched quite a few of our dreams come true. Along the way, we acquired many of the material possessions that seemed, at the time, to be prerequisites to success and happiness. But it wasn't until we'd been married for over two decades—and when our children prepared to take flight from our family's nest—that we started thinking seriously and systematically about the good life: what it means and how to achieve it.

It all started because of downsizing. And simplifying.

The year we were married, Ricky Skaggs recorded a song called "Simple Life". The lyrics to that song came to mind when, almost a quarter of a century later, our family began the intentional process of simplification. We sold our place in the country and moved into a smaller home on a much smaller lot. As we did, we were humming along with Ricky as we pondered what it means to live simply and well.

When the impulse to downsize began, it had to do with freeing up finances for upcoming life changes. We knew that we'd need to invest in Karen's new business. With two kids in high school, we could also see college expenses looming on the horizon. It wasn't just future concerns, either. We'd been struggling to live within our budget for a while, and life had become stressful and complicated. As we've counseled others before, families facing tight financial times really have only two options: decrease expenses or increase income. Because we were both already working as much as we could, cutting costs was the obvious choice for us. And our biggest expense was housing.

Ken warily brought up the subject of a move as a "what if," fully expecting resistance from the whole family. We dearly loved our home's secluded, retreat-like setting among woods and fields. We'd even told friends that we'd retire there and perhaps even be buried on the property when we died! Therefore it came as a surprise for Ken to hear positive responses from everyone. It turned out that we all had a desire to streamline and simplify.

Because we talk openly about finances as a family, the kids caught our excitement at the prospect of having some "margin" or wiggle-room in the budget. Somehow the urge to scale things back caused us to begin thinking differently about our lifestyle. It was as if we'd awakened some dormant minimalist gene within ourselves, something that dared us to consider how little we could live with, not how much we could accumulate. That's what got us started thinking about "the good life": how we should define it and how we could achieve it.

After some careful planning, we did downsize to a smaller home, and things worked out for the best, just as we'd hoped. Karen and I are now empty-nesters; we're comfortably settled into our house; and, we are happy for the time and resources that the move freed up. The process of simplifying our lives worked well for us, and we believe that it will work for you, too. But popular culture would have you believe otherwise.

The world has its own particular definition of the good life, a definition that we've come to distrust. The world, with its vast multitude of media messengers, tells us that the best way to enjoy life—perhaps the only way—is to acquire more stuff. The world tells us that more is better and that the person who dies with the most toys wins. This message, of course, is a complete fabrication, a total fiction created by savvy marketers who are focused on their own sales reports, not our own wellbeing.

As we began to think more carefully about the *real* components of happiness and contentment, the idea for this book came into focus. On the pages that follow, we'll share fourteen essential principles for living an authentically good life. These principles have surprisingly little to do with materialism. Instead, they have to do with timeless values like faith, trust, optimism, and obedience.

You may believe that the good life is actually a mirage, or a faraway destination that you'll finally reach on some fine day in the distant future. If that's what you're thinking, think again. You can claim the good life *now* if you focus on the things that really matter. Does that mean that you'll be blissfully happy twenty-four hours a day for the rest of your life? No, that's not The Good Life as we see it, and it's not the abundant life Jesus talks about in John 10:10. In fact, The Good Life has very little to do with material possessions. It's not about the things we own; it's about the attitudes we hold, the beliefs we live by, the blessings we count, the love we hold in our hearts, and the faith that we have in a loving God. These are the things that really matter, and if we must simplify our lives in order to see these blessings more clearly, well, that's a very small price to pay.

14 COMMON-SENSE PRINCIPLES FOR LIVING THE GOOD LIFE *NOW*

1. **You can enjoy The Good Life—beginning now—and you should:** Don't wait for tomorrow. Start living The Good Life today. After all, each day is a gift from above, so treat it that way. Make up your mind that this day—and every other day, for that matter—can be, and should be, a cause for celebration.

2. **You can't buy The Good Life because it's not for sale:** The world spews out messages that money and possessions can buy happiness. These messages are false and dangerous to your emotional, spiritual, and financial health. Act accordingly.

3. **To experience The Good Life, you must stay morally and spiritually grounded:** The spiritual compass that God planted in your heart always points directly to The Good Life. The world often points you in a different direction. Trust the compass.

4. **Strive for simplicity:** When in doubt, choose the simpler route. Less is, indeed, more, and simplicity is, as the old saying goes, genius. Act accordingly.

5. **Count your blessings, not your hardships:** Focus on the roses, not the thorns. And don't waste time complaining. Complaining doesn't work anyway, so why waste your breath?

6. **Stop comparing yourself to other people:** Theodore Roosevelt said "Comparison is the thief of joy." Don't let the thief steal your joy.

7. **Learn to manage your money before your money manages you:** It's hard to experience The Good Life while the bill collector is pounding on the door. So take a disciplined approach to your spending and do whatever it takes to avoid mountains of debt.

8. **Be as generous as you can be, and then some:** Media marketers want you to focus on getting. God wants you to focus on giving. So, give till it hurts a little. As the old saying goes, the more you give, the more you'll get.

9. **Make peace with your past:** Whatever it is, get over it. Accept the unchangeable past and focus on the thing you can change: your future.

10. **Learn to worry less and trust God more:** You can spend the rest of your life worrying about things that might or might not happen. But why should you? Instead, teach yourself to be a realistic optimist, not a perpetual pessimist.

11. **Get enough rest and keep recharging your battery:** Get enough sleep; take time for yourself; take a vacation when you need it; learn how to unwind from the daily grind; and spend a few minutes every day with God. He wants to renew your spirit; your job is to let Him.

12. **Learn to control your thoughts (before they control you):** You won't experience The Good Life if your thoughts are constantly barking out bad instructions. So, it's imperative that you learn to monitor your thoughts and shepherd them in the right direction.

13. **Celebrate every season of life:** Throughout life your circumstances will most certainly change, but God's love never changes and neither do His promises. Rely on those promises in every season of life.

14. **Put God in His rightful place: first place:** God deserves first place in your life...and you deserve the experience of putting Him there.

AUTHORS' NOTE

In many instances—but not in every instance—we've chosen to capitalize the phrase The Good Life. When we capitalize these words, we are referring, not to "the good life" as defined by modern media, but instead to the authentic, simplified, faith-based life described in the pages of God's holy Word.

YOU CAN ENJOY THE GOOD LIFE–BEGINNING NOW–AND YOU SHOULD

This is the day which the LORD has made;
let us rejoice and be glad in it.

PSALM 118:24 NASB

The Good Life. It's a familiar phrase that evokes thoughts of happiness, contentment, and freedom from want. And, it's an expression that has been woven so completely into the modern mindset that most of us simply take the phrase for granted and spend very little time thinking about what it really means. Instead of thinking critically about ways to define what The Good Life actually entails—and instead of maintaining a laser-like focus on the steps required to achieve it—we become so absorbed by the demands of everyday life that we simply do each day's work and assume that better days will magically appear "someday."

While waiting for better days to arrive, far too many people seem content to drift through life, earning a paycheck, making ends meet, keeping a roof over their heads, and living for the weekend. Caught in the gears of the daily grind, they often talk about making a better life for themselves—or they spend idle hours dreaming about it—but they never quite get around to experiencing it. Instead of defining their goals and aspirations, they drift. Instead of living fully in the present moment, they focus on a mythical pot of gold at the end of some ill-defined mythical rainbow. Instead of facing reality and doing something about it, they daydream about a sudden windfall, or about winning the lotto, or receiving an unexpected inheritance. Instead of making up their minds that the best day to start living the good life is this day, they convince themselves that their lives will improve gradually over time. So they wait for the good times to arrive of their own accord. But unfortunately, people who make these sorts of assumptions may be in for a very long wait.

On the pages that follow, we'll suggest a different plan. Instead of waiting passively for your future to unfold, we'll ask you to start building a better life—*your* Good Life—now, not later. We'll challenge you to think carefully about your own situation: what it is today and what it should be tomorrow. We'll ask you to think critically about the steps you must take along your journey, and we'll ask you to think carefully about the bad habits or material possessions you may need to jettison along the way. And, we'll explore time-tested ways to maximize your joy by minimizing your distractions.

This text relies heavily on principles that can be found in a book like no other: the Holy Bible. The truths contained in God's Word are never out of date, so the Bible still serves as the best possible instruction book for achieving The Good Life and maintaining it. We have attempted, to the best of our abilities, to convey the biblical wisdom that we believe is essential to every well-lived life, including yours. Building upon the foundation of God's Word, we have also addressed the most important common-sense strategies that we believe can transform your day *and* your life.

So, if you're ready to improve your life by simplifying it, read on. And as you do, consider these pages to be a roadmap to the good life that God has planned for you and yours. As you read, think, learn, work, and pray, and don't be afraid to ask the Lord for His blessings. When you do, you'll be blessed in countless ways that you never expected. So with no further ado, let your personal journey—your personal exodus from the mundane to the miraculous—begin.

Now.

LIVE YOUR LIFE
WHILE YOU HAVE IT

*Live your life while you have it. Life is a splendid gift.
There is nothing small about it.*

FLORENCE NIGHTINGALE

*Fear not that thy life shall come to an end,
but rather fear that it shall never have a beginning.*

JOHN HENRY CARDINAL NEWMAN

*Each of us has one life to live on earth, and we
should cherish it in creative, imaginative ways.*

FRED ROGERS

*When I stand before God at the end of my life,
I would hope that I would not have
a single bit of talent left and could say,
"I used everything you gave me."*

ERMA BOMBECK

*God loves you and wants you to experience
peace and life—abundant and eternal.*

BILLY GRAHAM

*All of us tend to put off living. We are all dreaming
of some magical rose garden over the horizon
instead of enjoying the roses that are
blooming outside our windows today.*

DALE CARNEGIE

It's time to begin writing the story of your life.

DAVID JEREMIAH

THERE'S NO TIME LIKE THE PRESENT

Give your entire attention to what God
is doing right now, and don't get worked up
about what may or may not happen tomorrow.
God will help you deal with whatever
hard things come up when the time comes.

MATTHEW 6:34 MSG

This day, like every other day, is a gift from above. And whether we realize it or not, we all have countless reasons to be grateful. Yet on some days, when the demands of life threaten to overwhelm us, we don't feel much like rejoicing. Instead of celebrating God's glorious creation, we may find ourselves frustrated by the obligations of today and worried by the uncertainties of tomorrow. Instead of claiming God's peace, we try to keep up with the Joneses. Instead of treating each day as a priceless treasure, we're tempted to muddle along from problem to problem, solving a few, ignoring a few, and putting off the rest until "tomorrow."

Shakespeare's most familiar words on the topic can be found in *Macbeth*. The Bard of Avon understood the profound, one-way nature of time when he penned his protagonist's famous, and thoroughly jaded, soliloquy:

> Tomorrow, and tomorrow, and tomorrow,
> Creeps in this petty pace from day to day,
> To the last syllable of recorded time;
> And all our yesterdays have lighted fools
> The way to dusty death. Out, out, brief candle!
> Life's but a walking shadow, a poor player,
> That struts and frets his hour upon the stage,
> And then is heard no more. It is a tale
> Told by an idiot, full of sound and fury,
> Signifying nothing.

Macbeth's words were profoundly pessimistic, but he did get one thing right: life *does* unfold day by day. The fact that life presents itself in single-day increments is both patently obvious and undeniably profound. It means that God's priceless gift—the gift of another day of life—comes with a use-by date: it expires at midnight.

So the challenge for each of us is simply this: How will we use this day? Will we invest it or will we squander it? Will we take it for granted, or will we treasure it? Will we use God's twenty-four-hour gift to improve our own lives and the lives of our loved ones? Or will we choose a different path? That choice, of course, belongs to each of us. And so, by the way, do the consequences.

Macbeth was the king of Scots, so we might logically presume that he, more than any of his subjects, could use his wealth and power to claim the good life. But his soliloquy clearly proves that life seemed, to him, a burden not a blessing. For Macbeth, life was a long, meaningless, futile string of yesterdays filled with sound and fury, nothing more. But the king of Scots was mistaken. Life here on earth should never be viewed as a meaningless journey from cradle to grave. Life is, instead, a grand adventure for those who are wise enough, and faithful enough, to make it so.

We experience life one moment at a time. The present is, indeed, a remarkably small slice of the infinite, here for an instant, gone in a flash. It is precisely because time travels in only one direction—with no return route back to yesterday—that each day should be viewed as a unique, one-of-a-kind opportunity to experience The Good Life now, not later.

So the first principle of experiencing The Good life is simply this:

You can enjoy The Good Life—beginning now—
and you should
(not tomorrow, not next week, next month, or next year).

Okay, we know what you may be thinking. You may be telling yourself that you're simply too busy, too tired, or too worried to enjoy The Good Life today. But if that's what you're telling yourself, you're wrong. Even if you're enduring tough times—even if you're anxious, or discouraged, or both—you can still find time to step back from the chaos, to settle yourself down, and to thank the Creator for more blessings than you can possibly count. And then, when you've managed to make an incomplete list of your blessings, you can begin thinking carefully and analytically about what The Good Life really means *to you*.

DEFINING THE GOOD LIFE: WHAT IT MEANS TO YOU

The search for The Good Life is as old as humanity and as new as tomorrow's next big thing. But what, precisely, are we searching for? Are we trying to accumulate mountains of stuff, or is there more to The Good Life than that? Are we striving to keep up with the Joneses, or to get ahead of them? Or is there more to The Good Life than that? Are we struggling to finance a lifestyle that requires us to borrow from tomorrow's paycheck in order to pay for today's non-essentials? Or is there more to The Good Life than that? If these questions seem straightforward to you—perhaps even simplistic—that's because they *are* straightforward and simplistic. But they are also vitally important questions that you deserve to ask, and to answer, for yourself.

So here's our question for you: how will *you* define The Good Life? And as you think about your response, consider how many things in this world are more important than material possessions. For example, your health is more important. Your sanity is more important. Your values are more important. Your family is more important. Your faith is more important. And that's a starter-list at best.

If you're genuinely searching for contentment, for happiness, for fulfillment, and more—if you're sincerely searching for The Good Life—then you must think carefully about what The Good Life really means to you. While you're at it, don't fall for the slick Madison Avenue sales pitches that bombard you with messages designed to fill your mind and empty your wallet. Instead, compose your own definition of The Good Life in the space provided here. And, remember that the best and most important things in life can't be denominated in dollars, euros, yen, pounds, or francs. The best things in life are much more important than that.

MAKE A LIST OF THE THINGS
THAT ARE MOST IMPORTANT TO YOU

In the space below, make a list of the things that are most important to you. Try to arrange these elements in the approximate order of their importance. And while you're at it, don't forget the essentials: faith, family, and health.

_____

_____

_____

_____

_____

_____

_____

_____

_____

_____

_____

DEFINE WHAT THE GOOD LIFE MEANS TO YOU

After listing the things that are most important to you, now it's time to compose your own personal definition of The Good Life. Try to make it concise but comprehensive. We suggest that you use a pencil because you'll probably want to refine this definition as your thoughts evolve.

_____

_____

_____

_____

_____

_____

_____

_____

_____

_____

_____

SOME FINAL THOUGHTS ABOUT LIFE WITH A CAPITAL L

*The life you have led doesn't need
to be the only life you'll have.*

ANNA QUINDLEN

Nobody's gonna live for you.

DOLLY PARTON

*Life is what we make it. Always has been.
Always will be.*

GRANDMA MOSES

*You can't control the length of your life—
but you can control its width and depth.*

JOHN MAXWELL

*When it is time to die, let us not discover
that we have never lived.*

HENRY DAVID THOREAU

*Don't waste your life on things
that have no eternal value.*

BILLY GRAHAM

YOU CAN'T BUY THE GOOD LIFE BECAUSE IT'S NOT FOR SALE

Don't be obsessed with getting more material things.
Be relaxed with what you have.

HEBREWS 13:5 MSG

Lots of folks try to buy happiness, but they never get what they pay for. Why? Because happiness isn't for sale at any price. No matter how hard you try—and no matter how much you buy—you can't purchase The Good Life. Period. Full stop.

You happen to live in a society that worships material possessions. While many of our churches are emptying out, the temples of commerce are bulging at the seams. So, whether you're walking through the mall or surfing the Internet, the sales messages are ubiquitous. Everywhere you turn, or so it seems, you're confronted with images designed to sell you something. Savvy merchandisers employ a variety of pitches, some subtle, some not, which are intended to pry you off the couch and into their stores.

If you find yourself wrapped up in the concerns of the material world, it's time to reorder your priorities by turning your thoughts to more important matters. And, it's time to begin storing up riches that will endure throughout eternity: the spiritual kind. Money, in and of itself, is not evil, but worshipping money is. So today, as you prioritize matters of importance in your life, remember that God is almighty, but the dollar is not.

*Money exerts a certain control over us
because it seems to hold out
so much false promise of happiness.*

JOHN PIPER

*People make a mistake in
believing they're going to be
in paradise if they have more money.*

MAHALIA JACKSON

*Money won't make you happy,
but everybody wants to
find out for themselves.*

ZIG ZIGLAR

TO YURT, OR NOT TO YURT...
THAT IS THE QUESTION.

In our family, the battle against materialism has been fought on several fronts. So, we're constantly looking for ways to economize. One day Karen came home and said (semi-seriously) that she wanted to live in a "yurt." A yurt is a circular, dome-like, canvas-covered structure with its origins in Mongolia. Some of our friends had stayed overnight in one at Cair Paravel Farm in Stanardsville, Virginia, and it looked like the simplest housing ever. According to the Cair Paravel blog, they had raised their yurt in one day with the help of a few brawny neighbors. The final product turned out to be 30 feet in diameter and 18 feet high at the center. Doing the math, we figured out that a yurt that size has about 1,200 square feet of living space. Although that seemed like plenty of floor space to us, we quickly realized there would be near-zero privacy in a tent-like home without real interior partitions. Maybe a yurt could have worked when the kids were babies, but not anymore!

Having gotten yurts out of our system, we began scoping out "tiny houses" such as the ones built by the Tumbleweed Tiny House Company in Sonoma, California. Those guys have plans for fully outfitted houses with kitchens, bathrooms, bedrooms, and living areas, all inside a structure with between 260 and 884 square feet of living space. Although some of their homes are constructed on trailers (for portability) they aren't RVs—they're real houses.

Studying the plans, Ken was fascinated with the dedication to conserving space. Once again, though, we sensed that no matter how amazing the house, fitting ourselves and two teens into a pint-sized abode wasn't going to work. We decided that, at least for us, a downsized domicile was more fun to imagine than to live in.

Instead of the tiny house, we moved into a reasonably sized (and reasonably priced) ranch home in a nearby subdivision. As part of the move, we gave away or sold much of the stuff that had filled our garage, a separate storage building, and a rented storage unit. Downsizing was hard work, but it paid off.

After the move, we discovered that our new home took less energy to heat and cool, less time to keep clean, and less effort to mow and maintain the yard. We not only saved money, we also saved time. Since our downsizing, we've had more time to sit on the deck, to slow down the pace of life, and to enjoy our lives together as a family.

MATERIALISM 101: THE MARKETERS WANT YOU TO BE DISSATISFIED

Highly paid marketing gurus understand a simple truth, and you should understand it, too. The marketing experts realize that one of the best ways to sell you something is to make you dissatisfied with your current situation. Toward that end, they create advertisements that deliver a subtle but unmistakable message: they try to convince you that your stuff isn't good enough, and you deserve better.

The marketers tell you that your car isn't good enough (even if it still runs perfectly).

They tell you that your house isn't nice enough (or big enough, or new enough).

They tell you that your clothes aren't hip enough, that your teeth aren't white enough, and that your skin isn't tight enough.

They even tell you that your mattress isn't hard (or soft) enough.

If you take these messages to heart, you'll find yourself constantly searching for—and oftentimes paying for—the next big thing. And you may even go into debt for the privilege. But oftentimes the stuff you buy doesn't bring happiness, contentment, or satisfaction. Instead, your newly acquired possessions leave you with more headaches than you deserve and less cash than you need to live on.

The solution, of course, is simply this: learn to be satisfied with the things you have and reject the notion that your stuff isn't good enough. There's an old familiar saying that says, "If it ain't broke, don't fix it." To improve that adage, we would like to make the following modification: "And, if it ain't broke, don't replace it."

MORE THOUGHTS ABOUT THE DANGERS OF MATERIALISM

If you are really a product of a materialistic universe, how is it that you don't feel at home there?

C. S. LEWIS

Contentment consists not in multiplying wealth but in subtracting desires.

THOMAS FULLER

Contentment is possible when we stop striving for more.

CHARLES SWINDOLL

It's sobering to contemplate how much time, effort, sacrifice, compromise, and attention we give to acquiring and increasing our supply of something that is totally insignificant in eternity.

ANNE GRAHAM LOTZ

You will not be in heaven two seconds before you cry out, why did I place so much importance on things that were so temporary? What was I thinking? Why did I waste so much time, energy, and concern on what wasn't going to last?

RICK WARREN

HOW MUCH DOES IT REALLY TAKE TO BE SATISFIED?

Turn on your TV and start scrolling through the channels, and you'll come across a veritable smorgasbord of advertisements. Many of these ads will proclaim, "Satisfaction Guaranteed!" But that claim may not mean what you think it means. You may be satisfied with the way the product performs, but the product may not bring *you* any additional *satisfaction*. In other words, the product may work as advertised, but you may not be demonstrably better off when it does.

How much stuff does it really take to make you happy? This is an important question, a question that only you can answer. And to help you answer it, consider what Jesus had to say about it when He delivered the Sermon on the Mount:

> Do not store up for yourselves treasures on earth, where moths and vermin destroy, and where thieves break in and steal. But store up for yourselves treasures in heaven, where moths and vermin do not destroy, and where thieves do not break in and steal. For where your treasure is, there your heart will be also.

The eye is the lamp of the body. If your eyes are healthy, your whole body will be full of light. But if your eyes are unhealthy, your whole body will be full of darkness. If then the light within you is darkness, how great is that darkness!

No one can serve two masters. Either you will hate the one and love the other, or you will be devoted to the one and despise the other. You cannot serve both God and money (Matthew 6:19–24 NIV).

YOU CAN'T SERVE TWO MASTERS

*If your desires be endless, your cares
and fears will be so, too.*

THOMAS FULLER

*Money is emphasized in Scripture simply because
our temptation to love it is inexplicably powerful.*

ERWIN LUTZER

*Riches have never yet given anybody
either peace or rest.*

BILLY SUNDAY

*There is an endless road, a hopeless maze,
for those who seek goods before they seek God.*

ST. BERNARD OF CLAIRVAUX

*What we possess often possesses us—
we are possessed by possessions.*

OSWALD CHAMBERS

*Unhappiness is not knowing what
we want and killing ourselves to get it.*

DON HEROLD

NONESSENTIAL MAJOR PURCHASES THAT YOU DON'T ABSOLUTELY, POSITIVELY NEED RIGHT NOW

In the space below, make a list of major purchases that you don't absolutely, positively need right now. The list may include a new car, new furniture, new appliances, a new wardrobe, or a bigger house.

_____

_____

_____

_____

_____

_____

_____

_____

_____

_____

_____

FOLLOW YOUR MORAL COMPASS

So I strive always to keep my
conscience clear before God and man.

ACTS 24:16 NIV

To experience The Good Life in capital letters, you'll need a clear conscience. That means you'll need to follow your moral compass, wherever it may lead. To do so, you must pay careful attention to the quiet inner voice that God has planted in your heart, and whenever that voice issues a stern warning, you must listen and obey.

In His infinite wisdom, the Lord has provided each of us with a conscience—you can think of it as an early-warning signal against danger, temptation, and sin—and He wants us to use it. But sometimes, we don't. Instead of listening to the subtle voice that warns us against disobedience or disaster, we're tempted to rush headlong into situations that we soon come to regret. A far better strategy, of course, is to stay on the right path and make midcourse corrections as we go, using our moral compasses all day, every day.

God's Word promises that He will reward good conduct and that He will bless those who obey Him. But the Lord also issues a clear and unambiguous warning to those who disregard His commandments. Wise men and women heed that warning. Count yourself among their number.

Over the years, we've witnessed people who tried to achieve The Good Life without the benefit of a moral compass. These misguided folks relied upon deception, or bullying, or outright dishonesty to get what they wanted. But, even if they achieved their goals, it was never enough. Why were they deprived of the joy they'd worked for, schemed for, and fought for? Because real joy comes not from a collection of material possessions or fame, or power, or fortune. Real joy springs from a heart that's right with the Creator.

Sometimes, of course, we feel as though we are trapped in situations that are "beyond our control," and we feel compelled to "go along with the crowd" even if it means betraying the conscience God has placed within our hearts. But if "the crowd" is headed in the wrong direction, we must resist the temptation to follow. As Oswald Chambers correctly observed, "We talk about circumstances that are 'beyond our control.' None of us have control over our circumstances, but we are responsible for the way we pilot ourselves in the midst of things as they are." Obviously, Pastor Chambers understood the need to follow his moral compass, and so should we.

Sometime soon, perhaps today, your inner voice will speak; when it does, listen carefully. The Lord may be trying to get a message through to you, and it's a message that you most certainly need to hear.

LISTEN CAREFULLY TO YOUR CONSCIENCE

Labor to keep alive that little spark of celestial fire called conscience.

GEORGE WASHINGTON

Conscience is God's presence in man.

EMANUEL SWEDENBORG

Our battles are first won or lost in the secret places of our will in God's presence, never in full view of the world.

OSWALD CHAMBERS

Conscience can only be satisfied if God is satisfied.

C. H. SPURGEON

Conscience is our wisest counselor and teacher, our most faithful and most patient friend.

BILLY GRAHAM

God desires that we become spiritually healthy enough through faith to have a conscience that rightly interprets the work of the Holy Spirit.

BETH MOORE

The Bible teaches that when we turn our backs on God and choose to disregard His moral laws there are inevitable consequences.

BILLY GRAHAM

Disobedience to conscience makes conscience blind.

C. S. LEWIS

He will easily be content and at peace, whose conscience is pure.

THOMAS À KEMPIS

TO EXPERIENCE THE GOOD LIFE, YOU MUST LIVE IN ACCORDANCE WITH YOUR BELIEFS

There can be no happiness if the things we believe in are different from the things we do.

Freya Stark

If you sincerely want to experience The Good Life, then you must make certain that your actions are consistent with your beliefs. Does that mean that all your choices will conform perfectly to your belief system? Certainly not. None of us are perfect, so we shouldn't expect perfection from ourselves, or for that matter, from anyone else. But when it comes to living in accordance with our beliefs, we should expect consistent effort, and we should strive, day in and day out, to live within the spiritual and behavioral guardrails established by the inner voice that God has placed in each of our hearts.

Talking about our beliefs is easy; living by them is considerably harder. Yet God warns us that speaking about faith is not enough; we must also live by faith. Simply put, our theology must be demonstrated, not only with words but, more importantly, with actions.

When you listen carefully to your conscience—and

when you follow it—you'll experience the spiritual abundance that the Creator has promised to those who hear His words and follow in the footsteps of His Son. But if you choose a different path, The Good Life will remain elusive.

Every new day presents a fresh opportunity to make sure that your actions are consistent with your beliefs. When you follow your conscience, you'll be glad you did. Very glad. No exceptions.

LIVE WHAT YOU BELIEVE

If I had given you any parting advice it would,
I think, all have been comprised in this one sentence:
to live up always to the best and highest you know.

HANNAH WHITALL SMITH

There are two things to do about the gospel:
believe it and behave it.

SUSANNA WESLEY

A disciplined conscience is a man's best friend.
It may not be his most amiable,
but it is his most faithful monitor.

HENRY WARD BEECHER

GUARD YOUR HEART

And the peace of God, which surpasses
all understanding, will guard your hearts
and minds through Christ Jesus.

PHILIPPIANS 4:7 NKJV

God loves you. He cares for you. And, He wants you to experience His abundance. But He also knows that your adversary is near, so He wants you to guard your heart against the distractions and temptations that can cause harm and suffering.

Every day, you're faced with an array of choices—more choices than you can count. You can do the right thing, or not. You can be prudent, or not. You can be humble, kind, and obedient, or not. And you can follow your conscience wherever it leads. Or not.

Today, the world will offer you countless opportunities to let down your guard and, by doing so, make needless mistakes that may injure you and your loved ones. So be watchful. Guard your heart by giving it to your heavenly Father. It is safe with Him.

*We know the truth, not only by reason,
but by the heart.*

BLAISE PASCAL

BEWARE OF DISTRACTIONS, TEMPTATIONS, AND ADDICTIONS

In the space below, make note of any distractions, temptations, time-wasters, or bad habits that have, heretofore, held you back or brought you down. Identifying these traps and snares is an important first step. Eliminating them from your life may be harder, but don't despair. With God all things are possible.

_____

_____

_____

_____

_____

_____

_____

_____

_____

_____

COUNT YOUR BLESSINGS, NOT YOUR HARDSHIPS

In everything give thanks; for this is
the will of God in Christ Jesus for you.

1 THESSALONIANS 5:18 NKJV

Here's a question worth pondering: If you sat down this very moment and began counting your blessings—*all of them*—how long would it take? When you stop to think about it, the answer is: "A *very* long time." First, you'd need to give thanks to the Creator, who, in His infinite wisdom, brought light out of darkness. You'd remember, and be grateful for, the difficult lives of your forebears who worked, struggled, and cared for a long line of descendants that now includes you. You'd be sure to count among your blessings every single friend, mentor, coach, or teacher who has offered you a word of encouragement or a helping hand. You'd be mindful that your blessings include life, freedom, family, friends, and talents, for starters. But, your greatest blessing—a gift that is yours for the asking—is God's grace.

We honor God, in part, by the genuine gratitude we

feel in our hearts for His blessings. Yet even the most saintly among us may forget to count our blessings from time to time. Instead of being grateful for the things we do have, we engage in unwarranted self-pity and fruitless regret. Why? Because we are imperfect human beings who are incapable of perfect gratitude. We're mere mortals with short memories when it comes to our blessings but elephant-like memories when it comes to our misfortunes. So, we count problems, not gifts. This method of counting, by the way, is a profoundly shortsighted way to evaluate our circumstances.

Even on life's darker days, we must try, as best we can, to keep count of God's gifts. We must rid our hearts of negative emotions and fill them, instead, with praise, with love, with hope, and with thanksgiving. To do otherwise is to be unfair to ourselves, to our loved ones, and to our Creator.

Today, begin making a list of your blessings. You most certainly will not be able to make a complete list, but take a few moments and jot down as many blessings as you can. Then, give thanks to the Giver of all good things: God. His love for you is eternal, as are His gifts. And it's never too soon—or too late—to offer Him thanks.

THERE'S NO TIME LIKE THE PRESENT TO COUNT YOUR BLESSINGS

*Do we not continually pass by blessings
innumerable without notice, and instead
fix our eyes on our trials and our losses?
And, do we not talk about our trials until we
almost begin to think we have no blessings at all?*

HANNAH WHITALL SMITH

*God is always trying to give good things to us,
but sometimes our hands are too full to receive them.*

ST. AUGUSTINE

*It is always possible to be thankful for what is given
rather than to complain about what is not given.
One or the other becomes a habit of life.*

ELISABETH ELLIOT

*Count your own blessings
and let your neighbor count his.*

JAMES THURBER

No duty is more urgent than that of returning thanks.

ST. AMBROSE

LET EVERY DAY
BE THANKSGIVING

As believers in a risen Christ, we know that we are blessed beyond measure. God sent His only Son to die for us. And, the Lord has given us the priceless gifts of eternal love and eternal life. We, in turn, are instructed to approach our heavenly Father with reverence and thanksgiving. But sometimes, in the crush of everyday living, we simply don't stop long enough to pause and thank Him for the countless blessings He has bestowed upon us.

When we slow down and express our gratitude to the One who made us, we enrich our own lives and the lives of those around us. That's one reason—but not the only reason—that thanksgiving should become a habit, a regular part of our daily routines. God has blessed us beyond measure, and we owe Him everything, including our eternal praise.

Are you a thankful person? Do you appreciate the gifts that God has given you? And, do you demonstrate your gratitude by being a faithful steward of the gifts and talents that you have received from your Creator? You most certainly should be thankful. After all, when you stop to think about it, God has given you more blessings than you can fully contemplate or accurately count. So the question of the day is this: will you thank your Heavenly Father . . . or will you spend your time and energy doing other things?

God is always listening—are you willing to say thanks? It's up to you, and the next move is yours.

Enter into His gates with thanksgiving,
and into His courts with praise.
Be thankful to Him, and bless His name.
For the Lord is good; His mercy is everlasting,
and His truth endures to all generations.

Psalm 100:4–5 NKJV

MAKE A PARTIAL LIST
OF YOUR BLESSINGS

In the space below, make a list of things you are thankful for. The list will be incomplete (of course), but don't let that fact slow you down. Instead, just make your list and then pray about it. When you survey the list below, you'll be reminded that God is, indeed, good and that you are richly blessed.

_____

_____

_____

_____

_____

_____

_____

_____

_____

STRIVE FOR SIMPLICITY

Better a little with the fear of the LORD
than great wealth with turmoil.

PROVERBS 15:16 NIV

It's no wonder that Mac McAnally made it to the Songwriter's Hall of Fame. He's the virtuoso who penned a song called "Simple Life," which is the very same tune that we heard in the early 1990s when Ricky Skaggs recorded it. Now, almost three decades after he composed his thought-provoking tune, McAnally's words seem more relevant than ever:

Simple life is the life for me,
A man and a wife and a family.
And the Lord up above who knows I'm tryin'
To live a simple life in a difficult time.

Here in the twenty-first century, it's easier to talk about simplicity than to achieve it. We're constantly being bombarded by messages that encourage us to buy more stuff and, as a result, to complicate our lives. These messages, which invade our senses when we're online, or watching TV, or listening to the radio, or even driving down the highway, are intended to sell us things, most of which we don't really need. But because the adverts are so persuasive, we find ourselves chasing after a near-endless assortment of goods and services, caught up in a rat race that has no winners.

Our society is in love with money and the things that money can buy. God is not. God cares about people, not possessions, and so must we. We must, to the best of our abilities, resist the mighty temptation to place possessions ahead of people.

So, how much stuff is too much stuff? Well, if your desire for stuff is getting in the way of your desire to know God, then you've got too much stuff—it's as simple as that.

American naturalist and author Henry David Thoreau was born in Concord, Massachusetts, on July 12, 1817. He published just two books during his lifetime: *A Week on the Concord and Merrimack Rivers* and his masterpiece, *Walden*. Thoreau also penned the essay "Civil Disobedience," which subsequently influenced social activists such as Gandhi and Martin Luther King Jr.

Thoreau died in 1862, and it was not until 1906 that his journals and writings were published in twenty volumes. Below, we consider a simple sampling of wisdom about the joys of simplicity, direct from the shores of Walden Pond.

HENRY DAVID THOREAU ON SIMPLICITY

The cost of a thing is the amount
of life that must be exchanged for it.

My greatest skill has been to want but little.

Our life is frittered away by detail… Simplify, simplify,
simplify… simplicity of life and evolution of purpose.

A man is rich in proportion to the things
he can afford to let alone.

Beware of all activities that require new clothes.

THINK LIKE A MINIMALIST

Lay not up for yourselves treasures upon earth, where
moth and rust doth corrupt, and where thieves break
through and steal: but lay up for yourselves treasures
in heaven, where neither moth nor rust doth corrupt,
and where thieves do not break through nor steal: for
where your treasure is, there will your heart be also.

MATTHEW 6:19–21 KJV

Minimalism: "A tool to rid yourself of life's excesses
in favor of focusing on what's important—so you can find
happiness, fulfillment, and freedom." This definition comes
from Joshua Fields Millburn and Ryan Nicodemus, authors
and bloggers known as "The Minimalists." They focus on
the concept of owning less in order to enjoy life more. They
are, in a sense, a couple of modern-day Thoreaus, encouraging us to buy less, to save more, to use what we have, and
to resist the temptation to purchase what we don't really
need. It's the process of taking away nonessentials—things
that inevitably add stress—in order to focus on things that
are much more important.

We are now empty-nesters. This time of transition has
given us an opportunity to take a look at our lives and
evaluate where we are and where we want to be. After careful

consideration, we've come to believe that a minimalistic approach to life is the surest way to experience the very best things that life has to offer.

Financial coaches will tell you there are only two ways to improve your financial condition—earn more or spend less. We've tried to do both in our family, but until recently, it's never been much fun to cut spending. Lately, however, we've been inspired by a simple, yet profound, thought: one of the surest ways to improve life is to simplify it.

For some folks, it's about living in a smaller house. For others, it's about eliminating debt. And, for others, it's about getting off the money merry-go-round by adopting a simpler lifestyle, slowing down from the rush, from the overspending, and from the complexity that inevitably accompanies overspending. The more we read, the more we want to embrace simplicity by intentionally pursuing new purposes and priorities.

Many minimalists give away or sell the majority of their current possessions, keeping only what they regularly use or what carries significant personal meaning. Their goal is to become aware of how the things they buy and own impact their lives and their decisions. While we sorted through and gave away many things when we downsized to our current house, we are still interested in doing more. We want to make more room for the non-tangible priorities of our family's life.

KAREN REMEMBERS A SIMPLER TIME

As I think about simplification, I find myself reminiscing about my childhood. It struck me recently that my parents were actually minimalists. In their case, however, it wasn't by choice; it was something they just did. They were the parents of seven children, raising their family on a small farm in the country. My father was a pastor. With a pastor's salary. So, Dad had to augment his income with other ventures: in addition to other part-time jobs, he was a school bus driver and a mason. We always had a big garden and grew our own food, including beef cattle and chickens. It was a necessary part of life. Although we didn't have luxuries, we were always warm, and we had plenty to eat and wear.

In spite of a lower income—and in spite of having to work hard for everything they had—my parents enriched our family life through intangible things, simple things that money could never buy. Here are a few of my parents' greatest gifts to our family, to their friends, and to the world:

***Hospitality**—I can remember many Sunday dinners with guests after church. My mother would* spend Saturdays baking pies and preparing for Sunday dinners. I also remember two older bachelors who would often stop by on Sunday evening, right around suppertime. They seemed lonely, and I suspect they enjoyed all the activity that resulted from a houseful of kids.

Generosity—One clear memory etched in my mind is from a very cold winter night. We had heard that the house across the hill had burned to the ground, and we knew there were a number of children in the family. While no one was hurt, they lost everything. I remember standing on the threshold of our front door while my mother handed someone several bags of clothes for those children. That's just one of many stories of their generosity. My parents always demonstrated quiet generosity, and they were never too busy to help a neighbor.

Beauty—My father loved gardening, especially growing flowers. Dad grew some of the prettiest roses, and knew them all by name. His mother, my grandma, also had a green thumb. Both thrifty gardeners, they would start root cuttings and dig up bulbs to give away and share with others.

Creativity—My mother has always loved quilts and enjoyed recycling fabric scraps to make beautiful creations that are as functional as they are lovely. She still quilts and donates to her local relief sale. It is her joy to be creative and to share her talents with others.

Rest—Other than cooking a meal and taking care of the animals, my parents always took a rest from work on Sundays. This was time for going to church, time for visiting with family, and, of course, time for a good Sunday afternoon nap. They knew the value of having a break from the day-to-day routine, and they understood the value of allowing their minds and bodies to be refreshed.

As I reflect on ways to practice minimalism, it isn't just about saving money or keeping expenses in check. It's also a way to maximize the intrinsic value of each day. The older I get, the more I appreciate my parents' lifestyle—the intangible fruits of simplicity. Although I cannot embrace every facet of minimalism, I can focus on the important things in life. All of us can, and I believe that all of us should.

But godliness with contentment is a great gain.
For we brought nothing into the world,
and we can take nothing out. But if we have
food and clothing, we will be content with these.
But those who want to be rich fall into temptation,
a trap, and many foolish and harmful desires,
which plunge people into ruin and destruction.

1 Timothy 6:6–9 HCSB

CHILDLIKE SIMPLICITY

There's a big difference between simplicity and simple-mindedness. The Bible warns us against simplemindedness, foolishness, and impulsivity. But God's Word does praise simplicity and the benefits of the simple life. In this context, simplicity means being authentic, plain-spoken, and natural, not complex or double-minded.

Simplicity means being honest and straightforward, being unwilling to deceive or mislead others with clever words or hidden agendas. It also means being real—being sensitive to our own feelings and expressing them honestly. Childlike simplicity means that we can experience our feelings instead of repressing them or hiding them. Brennan Manning, author of *The Ragamuffin Gospel*, describes this as the contrast between the inner child and the inner Pharisee.

He writes: "The inner child is aware of his feelings and uninhibited in their expression; the Pharisee edits feelings and makes a stereotyped response to life situations."

When we reject childlike simplicity, it's sometimes because we want to give the "expected" and "acceptable" response—whatever makes us look good. We shove our real feelings down and don't deal with them. Brennan Manning writes that "to dismiss our feelings is to fail to listen to the stirrings of the Spirit within our emotional life. Jesus listened."

In the Gospels we are told that Jesus was moved with the deepest emotions—His anger erupted, He was sad, grieved, frustrated, and enraged. Jesus was authentic and real. He was a man in a way that we've forgotten men can be: truthful, blunt, emotional, non-manipulative, sensitive, compassionate, and uninhibited. To be more like Jesus, we would do well to embrace a childlike simplicity.

KEEPING IT SIMPLE
REQUIRES DISCIPLINE

Albert Einstein famously said, "Make things as simple as possible, but not simpler." But in today's complicated world, that's easier said than done. You live in a world where simplicity is in short supply. Think for a moment about the complexity of your everyday life and compare it to the lives of ancestors who lived only a hundred short years ago. Certainly, you are the beneficiary of many technological innovations, but those innovations have a price: in all likelihood, your world is highly complex.

From the moment you wake up in the morning until the time you lay your head on the pillow at night, you are the target of an endless stream of advertising information. Each message is intended to grab your attention in order to convince you to purchase things you didn't know you needed (and probably don't!). And the pace of technology is ever-quickening, leaving you with the uneasy feeling that the more you learn about high-tech matters, the more you need to learn.

You probably have, at your fingertips, a broad range of communication tools that can both improve your life and monopolize your time. Communication with your fellow human beings has never been cheaper or easier. If you so choose, you can be part of a global communication network with billions of your fellow human beings posting images for your perusal. And, to complicate matters further, a general prosperity has settled over the land, and you, as a member of this prosperous generation, probably have more money than your forefathers to spend on things that you may not really need. More spending means more items cluttering the landscape of your life.

Ours is a complicated society, a highly competitive place where people and corporations vie for your attention, for your time, and for your dollars. Don't let them succeed in complicating your life. Unless you take firm control of your time and your life, you may be overwhelmed by an ever-increasing tidal wave of complexity that threatens your happiness. Your assignment, if you choose to accept it, is to sort through the clutter, separate important matters from unimportant ones, and, in doing so, invest your time and effort on the things that are important to you and your loved ones. When you do, you'll be blessed...and so will they.

MORE THOUGHTS ABOUT THE JOYS OF SIMPLICITY

Less is more.

LUDWIG MIES VAN DER ROHE

Teach us to delight in simple things.

RUDYARD KIPLING

It is the simple things of life that make living worthwhile, the sweet fundamental things such as love and duty, work and rest, and living close to nature.

LAURA INGALLS WILDER

When we recall the past, we usually find that it is the simplest things—not the great occasions—that, in retrospect, give off the greatest glow of happiness.

BOB HOPE

Everything should be made as simple as possible, but not simpler.

ALBERT EINSTEIN

Contentment consists not in multiplying wealth but in subtracting desires.

THOMAS FULLER

KEEP STRIVING FOR SIMPLICITY

In the space below, jot down specific steps you can take to simplify—and thereby improve—your life. Then, put a target date by each item on your list.

_____

_____

_____

_____

_____

_____

_____

_____

_____

_____

_____

_____

_____

STOP COMPARING YOURSELF TO OTHER PEOPLE

You must not covet your neighbor's house…
or anything else that belongs to your neighbor.

EXODUS 20:17 NLT

I t's simple: If you make a habit of comparing yourself to other people, you won't be happy. You'll be jealous. You'll be envious. You'll be dissatisfied with your circumstances, with your surroundings, and yourself. But you won't be happy, at least not for long. We know this to be true from firsthand experience.

KEN'S EXPERIENCE WITH COMPARISONS

A few summers ago, our family stayed for several days at the posh and elegant Gaylord National Resort and Convention Center on the National Harbor near Washington, DC. We were guests there because it was the location of that year's Scripps National Spelling Bee, in which our son was a contestant. The place dazzled us. The resort has two thousand luxurious rooms, a nineteen-story glass atrium overlooking the Potomac River, a junior-Olympic indoor pool, and lush indoor gardens. The atrium even has a "performing" water fountain that synchronizes lights, music, and fifty-foot jets of water to create a memorable show each night.

As thrilled as our family was to be there, I felt uncomfortable and out of place as soon as we arrived. As we pulled our old minivan under the vast, arched concrete canopy at the hotel's entrance, I realized that every other vehicle in sight was shiny, new, and expensive. Suddenly, I didn't want the smartly dressed valets, bellhops, and doormen to approach my dusty and slightly dented family van. I was so intent on avoiding them that I dropped off the family, drove to a satellite parking lot, and carried our bags across the property myself. I looked like a pack mule.

Karen didn't understand my actions, and I couldn't explain myself right away. It took a few minutes to figure out what had made me feel so unwelcome. It certainly wasn't the hotel staff or the other spelling bee attendees. They were warm and friendly. What made me flee the hotel entry was a feeling of shame that washed over me as I compared my vehicle to everyone else's.

Theodore Roosevelt is credited with saying that "comparison is the thief of joy." That saying held true for me at the Gaylord resort. For years, we'd happily driven older cars with higher mileage, preferring to wear vehicles out rather than having a car payment. I'd felt good about my financial choices and had no qualms about what I drove, but on that day at the National Harbor, my contentment disappeared. In comparison to the other Spelling Bee families, we looked like impoverished bumpkins.

I thought of this situation recently when a friend wanted to tour the new house we have under construction. We've had fun stopping in every few days to watch the building progress, but I felt a sense of dread as I awaited our friend's visit. Our visitor had built a very nice home not long before, and I feared what he would say when he saw our future home. In comparison to his place, ours was small and simple, with few extra amenities.

Once again, comparison was the thief of joy and the enemy of contentment. I'd been excited about our house until I compared it with his. As I realized what I was feeling, I also recognized the impulse that was rising up within me: to spend more money on stuff that would impress people.

I could think of several other times I'd felt that impulse. On a recent visit to the Congressional offices in Washington, DC, I'd worn business attire that was clean, neat, pressed, and coordinated. I was feeling fine about myself until I looked around at the others walking the halls with me. In comparison to the lobbyists, legislators, and aides, I felt almost sloppy. No doubt about it—I needed to buy a new suit!

What's behind the intense desire to spend money on something we don't need in order to impress people we don't even know? It's insidious, irrational, and very, very powerful. And it all seems to begin when we start comparing ourselves with others.

A family friend with many children told me that his kids used to be happy at Christmas to get one carefully selected book, one high-quality toy, and one nice item of clothing. With their big family, that arrangement was the best way to stretch their gift budget. Unfortunately, the contentment faded after they compared notes with other children in the neighborhood. The words of one neighbor boy were particularly discouraging. "Man," he said, "your Christmas stunk, didn't it? You should see what I got this year." It was a stark comparison that left our *friend's kids feeling embarrassed. The gifts that they'd found so pleasing no longer felt like "enough."*

I can only think of one antidote to the poison that often sickens our hearts when we compare ourselves and our situations with that of others, and that's gratitude. To avoid the depressing emptiness of feeling "less than," we can stop and think about all that we have and are. There is so much for which we can be thankful—from health and relationships to food and a warm place to sleep. Gratitude leads to contentment. I agree with Christian speaker and teacher Joyce Meyer, who says that "there is no happier person than a truly thankful, content person." And, she was right: No matter our circumstances, we're always more content—and we always experience more joy—if we refuse to compare ourselves (and our stuff) with other people (and their stuff).

STAY HUMBLE

Humility is not a very popular concept in today's culture. The word humility comes from the root word *humus*—earth, ground, dirt. It implies submission, servanthood, and a low position. That's antithetical to today's thinking. Here in the twenty-first century, we're supposed to focus on things like self-esteem, self-care, self-actualization, and self-help. (Did you notice that every single one of these hyphenated phrases begins with the word "self"?).

And when we've finished pumping ourselves up, we're supposed to share the new-and-improved versions of ourselves with the world on social media. So we post highlight reels on our favorite platforms, carefully picking out the best shots to share with friends, with neighbors, and with a few billion other folks (if they're interested). Whether we like it or not, we now live in the world of Facebook, Snapchat, and Instagram. These twenty-first century behemoths are useful tools for communicating with loved ones in faraway places, but they become destructive if they encourage us to focus on ourselves, not on others.

God's Word clearly teaches that we, as Christians, are called to be humble servants, not social-media rock stars. So, our challenge is simply this: How do we find a healthy balance between self-care and self-aggrandizement? The answer, according to God, is that we should gain a sense of self-worth through humble service, not self-glorification.

Pride is both subtle and dangerous. So, as thoughtful believers—and as responsible human beings who sincerely want to make the world a better place—we must be on guard. Even though God's Word clearly warns us that pride is hazardous to our spiritual health, we're still tempted to crow about our accomplishments, and to overstate them.

We're tempted to puff ourselves up by embellishing our victories and concealing our defeats. We're tempted to display the highlight reels and delete the bloopers. But in truth, all of us are mere mortals who have many more reasons to be humble than prideful.

As Christians who are the recipients—now and eternally—of God's grace, how can we be prideful? The answer, of course, is that if we are honest with ourselves and with our Creator we simply can't be boastful. We must, instead, be filled with humble appreciation for the things God has done. Our good works are minuscule compared to His. Whatever happens, the Lord deserves the credit, not us. And, if we're wise, we'll give Him all the credit He deserves.

ENVY IS DANGEROUS AND DESTRUCTIVE

Let us not be desirous of vainglory,
provoking one another, envying one another.

GALATIANS 5:26 KJV

God's Word warns us that envy is sin. And, as Christians, we have absolutely no reason to be envious of any people on earth. After all, because of our relationship with Christ, we are already recipients of the greatest gift in all creation: God's grace. We have been promised the gift of eternal life through God's only begotten Son, and we must count that gift as our most precious possession.

St. John Chrysostom observed, "As a moth gnaws a garment, so does envy consume a man." And he was right; envy, left unchecked, gradually eats away at our souls. So here's a simple suggestion that is guaranteed to bring you happiness: fill your heart with God's love, God's promises, and God's Son . . . and when you do so, leave no room for envy and no time to compare yourself to others.

As the recipient of God's grace, you have every reason to celebrate life. After all, God has promised you the opportunity to receive His abundance and His joy—in fact, you have the opportunity to receive those gifts right now. But if you allow envy to gnaw away at the fabric of your soul, you'll find that joy remains elusive. So if you genuinely want to experience The Good Life, focus on the marvelous things that God has done for you, not the things He may—or may not—have done for other people. And if you want a simple, surefire formula for a happier, healthier life, here it is: Count your own blessings and let your neighbors count theirs. It's the godly way to live.

STOP COMPARING YOURSELF TO OTHERS

It is comfortable to know that we are responsible to God and not to man. It is a small matter to be judged of man's judgment.

LOTTIE MOON

It took me a long time not to judge myself through someone else's eyes.

SALLY FIELD

Everybody must learn this lesson somewhere— it costs something to be what you are.

SHIRLEY ABBOT

Nobody can make you feel inferior without your consent.

ELEANOR ROOSEVELT

Outside appearances, things like the clothes you wear or the car you drive, are important to other people but totally unimportant to God. Trust God.

MARIE T. FREEMAN

We forfeit three-fourths of ourselves
in order to be like other people.

ARTHUR SCHOPENHAUER

You don't have to look like everybody else
to be acceptable and be accepted.

FRED ROGERS

By the grace of God you are what you are;
glory in your selfhood, accept yourself
and go on from there.

WILFERD PETERSON

Face your deficiencies and acknowledge them;
but do not let them master you. Let them
teach you patience, sweetness, insight.
When we do the best we can,
we never know what miracle is wrought
in our life, or in the life of another

HELEN KELLER

Resolve to be thyself, and know that
he who finds himself loses his misery.

MATTHEW ARNOLD

COMPARING YOURSELF TO OTHERS IS AN INTELLECTUAL AND SPIRITUAL DEAD END

In the space below, make a list of ways that you compare yourself to other people. Perhaps you're envious of someone's bigger house, newer car, or bigger bank balance. Or you may come up with other things that make you feel inferior or envious. Don't hold back; be honest with yourself. Then, when you've completed the list, spend a few minutes thinking about the negative consequences of comparing yourself to other people. And finally, pray about your list and ask God to help you focus on His gifts to you, not the gifts He's given to others.

_____

_____

_____

_____

_____

_____

_____

BE GENEROUS WITH YOUR TIME, YOUR TREASURE, AND YOUR TALENTS

Freely you have received, freely give.

MATTHEW 10:8 NKJV

I tell you the truth, whatever you did for one of the least of these brothers of mine, you did for me.

MATTHEW 25:40 NIV

Throughout the Bible, in both the Old Testament and the New, God instructs us to be generous, joyful, thoughtful givers. In fact, the theme of generosity is woven into the very fabric of God's Word. Time and again, the Lord instructs us to give generously—and cheerfully—to those in need. And He promises that when we do give of our time, our talents, and our resources, we will be blessed.

Jesus was the perfect example of generosity. He gave us everything, even His earthly life, so that we, His followers, might receive abundance, peace, and eternal life. He was always charitable, always kind, and always willing to help "the least of these." In fact, our Lord's words remind us that when we find ways to help the neediest among us, we are, quite literally, helping Him.

We can never equal Christ's generosity—we can never even come close. But, if we want to follow in His footsteps, we must try to follow His example: we, too, must be generous.

Sometime today, you'll encounter someone who needs a helping hand or a word of encouragement. When you encounter a person in need, think of yourself as Christ's ambassador. And remember that whatever you do for the least of these, you also do for Him.

WHAT GOD'S WORD SAYS ABOUT GENEROSITY

Freely you have received; freely give.

MATTHEW 10:8 NIV

So let each one give as he purposes in his heart,
not grudgingly or of necessity;
for God loves a cheerful giver.

2 CORINTHIANS 9:7 NKJV

You should remember the words of the Lord Jesus:
"It is more blessed to give than to receive."

ACTS 20:35 NLT

If you have two coats, give one to the poor.
If you have food, share it with those who are hungry.

LUKE 3:11 NLT

Whenever we have the opportunity,
we should do good to everyone,
especially to those in the family of faith.

GALATIANS 6:10 NLT

KEN'S OBSERVATIONS ABOUT THE GIVE-AWAY EXPERIMENT

A few years ago, we conducted a financial experiment. It was Karen's idea. After reading a book about what the Bible says about money, she suggested that our budget should include a certain amount of "give-away money." The experiment would test the idea that giving money away can bring greater joy than simply having money to spend. So every other week, we each took a certain amount, in cash, to give away to whomever we wanted. The only rule was we had to give it, not spend it.

Karen was all-in, but I have to admit that I was somewhat skeptical. When I did the math in my head, I realized that the amount we'd be giving away in a year was sizable. It would easily fund the purchase of some really nice stuff. We could pay for a beach vacation or a cruise. More practically, we could cover expensive car repairs or help pay for our kids' braces.

Perhaps because of this resistant attitude, I usually held onto my cash for a while before I figured out what to do with it. I wanted God to take the lead, and I wanted to give wisely. So I began looking around for people and situations, searching for needs.

It wasn't easy. For one thing, I realized that I spent most of my time with people who needed very little. But I faced an even bigger challenge: I realized that when I saw a potential need, my first motivation wasn't to help the other person; it was to silently judge that person for managing his or her life poorly. Every few days, however, I would stumble upon the extra cash in my wallet, remember Karen's experiment, and focus on opportunities to give. This other-centeredness soon had an effect. My self-admitted selfishness, my self-proclaimed "inner miser" had an attitude shift. As days passed, I discovered the extra cash in his wallet didn't look like lunch money or grocery money anymore. Instead, it began to look like a way to be kind, to show compassion and to focus on others.

The "give-away money" bought gas for a mother commuting between one child at a distant hospital and one child at home. It helped buy roofing cement and supplies to patch an elderly lady's leaky roof. It bought a pizza dinner for a stressed-out couple trying to care for a couple of sick kids. It helped a short-term missionary fund his trip. Sometimes the recipient knew the gift was from Karen and me, but whenever I could, I gave anonymously. Either way, I experienced joy. Meanwhile, my judgmental attitude slowly dissolved into something that felt more like empathy, and my heart opening up to the world around me.

Proverbs 11:24–25 (NIV) says, "One person gives freely, yet gains even more; another withholds unduly, but comes to poverty. A generous person will prosper; whoever refreshes others will be refreshed." And we can attest, from personal experience, that this promise is true. Looking back on our give-away experiment, we realize it is spiritual poverty to close our hearts to needs we see, needs that God may be nudging us to help meet. It is poverty to horde wealth without faith that God will provide.

Now we truly feel wealthier every time we give. Letting go of cash helps us to let go of the "stuff" of this world and grab onto things that matter more, such as relationships, belief, trust, charity, and hope. It makes us grateful for the abundant blessings we have been given. Like the tithes and offerings we give, this experiment turns our hearts toward God as our provider. We trust Him more. And we're enjoying spiritual freedom as materialism loosens its grip on us. We engage more in the lives of people around us as we seek to be a blessing. As a couple, our conversations about giving bring energy and encouragement into otherwise mundane conversations about money. The proverb promises that whoever refreshes others will be refreshed, and for us, it's proved true.

MORE THOUGHTS ABOUT GENEROSITY

The world asks, "What does a man own?"
Christ asks, "How does he use it?"

ANDREW MURRAY

God does not need our money.
But you and I need the experience of giving it.

JAMES DOBSON

In Jesus the service of God and the service
of the least of the brethren were one.

DIETRICH BONHOEFFER

As faithful stewards of what we have, ought we not
to give earnest thought to our staggering surplus?

ELISABETH ELLIOT

We must not slacken our efforts to do good to all,
especially to those with needs that will not be met if
we fail in our common task of service to humanity.

DANNY THOMAS

Christian life consists in faith and charity.

MARTIN LUTHER

MAKE THE MOST OF YOUR TALENTS

Life is like a ten-speed bike.
Most of us have gears we never use.

CHARLES SCHULZ

Giving away money is one way of demonstrating generosity, but it's not the only way. You can also be generous with your talents, and you should be. After all, God gave you a particular set of skills, and put you in a particular place, at a particular time, with a particular purpose. Now, it's your turn to demonstrate your gratitude for those gifts by using them for the glory of His kingdom.

In the twenty-fifth chapter of Matthew, Jesus tells the "Parable of the Talents." In it, He describes a master who leaves his servants with varying amounts of money (talents). When the master returns, some servants have put their money to work and earned more, to which the master responds, "Well done, good and faithful servant! You have been faithful with a few things; I will put you in charge of many things. Come and share your master's happiness!" (Matthew 25:21 NIV)

But the story does not end so happily for the unwise servant who did nothing with the single talent he had been given. In responding to the servant's shortsightedness, the master had great reproach: "You wicked, lazy servant!" (Matthew 25:26 NIV). Christ's message is clear: we are to use our talents, not waste them.

Your unique assortment of talents and opportunities comprises a treasure on temporary loan from God. He intends that you give generously, to serve His children and enrich the world. Value the gift that God has given you, nourish it, make it grow, and share it with the world. Then, when you meet your Master face-to-face, you, too, will hear those wonderful words, "Well done, good and faithful servant!… Come and share your Master's happiness!"

If we accept that Life is a gift,
it seems to me we must then accept the notion
that we ought to do something with this gift.

DOROTHY COTTON

YOUR THOUGHTS ABOUT THE JOYS– AND REWARDS–OF GENEROSITY

In the space below, take a few moments to jot down your thoughts about the joys and rewards that accrue to people (like you) who give generously of their time, their talents, and their treasure. Think about ways that cheerful generosity can contribute to The Good Life. And as you write, remember the promise made in Proverbs 11:25: "A generous person will prosper; whoever refreshes others will be refreshed."

_____

_____

_____

_____

_____

_____

_____

_____

_____

LEARN TO MANAGE YOUR MONEY (BEFORE IT MANAGES YOU)

Good planning and hard work lead to
prosperity, but hasty shortcuts lead to poverty.

PROVERBS 21:5 NLT

You don't need to be a millionaire to experience The Good Life. Time and again, the old adage has been proven true: "Money can't buy happiness." But with that caveat in mind, it's also worth noting that constant struggles with money can make life difficult, complicated, and stressful. Perhaps that's why God's Word gives us clear instructions about money: how to earn it, how to prioritize it, and how to manage it.

Entire books have been written about money management (in fact, we've written one ourselves), but in this text, we'll keep it simple by addressing six rock-solid principles for taking control of your finances before your finances take control of you.

MONEY-MANAGEMENT PRINCIPLE #1: DON'T WORSHIP MONEY

For the love of money is a root of all kinds of evil.
Some people, eager for money,
have wandered from the faith
and pierced themselves with many griefs.

1 TIMOTHY 6:10 NIV

We'll start with the most important money management principle of all, which is simply this: Don't worship money. This principle is straightforward, easy-to-understand, and nonnegotiable. Simply put, we can worship God, or we can worship money, but we can't worship both.

If we wish to enjoy The Good Life, we cannot let greed or materialism conquer us. Why? Because the moment that we begin to worship money is the moment that we begin to sow discontentment in our souls.

God's Word instructs us to worship Him and only Him (Exodus 20:3), yet we are sorely tempted to do otherwise. We are tempted to seek fulfillment from other sources including, but not limited to, material possessions. But if we do so, we create problems for ourselves and for our loved ones.

Of course savvy media marketers are constantly trying to

convince us that money alone will bring us peace, contentment, and happiness. These messages are often subtle but always untrue. Genuine abundance is not a function of worldly possessions or personal gratification; genuine abundance is a function of our relationship with God. Period. So we must remember that the almighty dollar isn't really almighty; only the almighty God fits that description.

Life is not a matter of dollars and cents, houses and lands, or financial achievement. Greed must not be allowed to make man the slave of wealth.

BILLY GRAHAM

MONEY MANAGEMENT PRINCIPLE #2: WORK HARD AND ALWAYS GIVE YOUR BEST

In all the work you are doing, work the best you can. Work as if you were doing it for the Lord, not for people.

COLOSSIANS 3:23 NCV

Working at your job, earning a living wage, and caring for your family requires effort and plenty of it. And that's perfectly okay with God. In his second letter to the Thessalonians, Paul warns, "If any would not work, neither should he eat" (3:10 KJV). And the book of Proverbs proclaims, "One who is slack in his work is brother to one who destroys" (18:9 NIV). In short, God has created a world in which diligence is rewarded but sloth is not. So, whatever it is that you choose to do, do it with commitment, excitement, and vigor.

Hard work is not simply a proven way to advance your career; it's also part of God's plan for you. God did not create you for a life of mediocrity; He created you for far greater things. The Lord will never give you more than He knows you can handle. And of this you can be sure: God has big plans for you if you possess a loving heart and willing hands.

Work is a blessing. God has so arranged the world that work is necessary, and He gives us hands and strength to do it. The enjoyment of leisure would be nothing if we had only leisure.

ELISABETH ELLIOT

God gives talent. Work transforms talent into genius.

ANNA PAVLOVA

The best preparation for good work tomorrow is to do good work today.

ELBERT HUBBARD

MONEY MANAGEMENT PRINCIPLE #3: MAKE A BUDGET, UNDERSTAND YOUR BUDGET, AND LIVE WITHIN YOUR MEANS

Unfortunately, most people don't have a written budget. A budget is an obvious, straightforward, easy-to-understand way of managing money, but it's a tool that most people refuse to use. Why? Oftentimes, it's because these folks are afraid of the things that their budgets might reveal. Members of the non-budget crowd tell themselves that they're simply "too busy to budget" or that they're "bad with numbers." But in reality, these people are worried that their budgets might contain bad news; they're fearful that the cold hard facts may be too cold and too hard to take. Such opinions are misguided because, when it comes to money matters, ignorance is never bliss.

Creating a budget is relatively easy. Living by that budget can be considerably harder because life-on-a-budget demands discipline and self-sacrifice. But if you're searching for peace and prosperity, it's imperative that you have a written plan that reflects your monthly income and expenses. And it's imperative that you do whatever it takes—and that you make whatever financial sacrifices are necessary—to live within your means.

MORE THOUGHTS ABOUT LIVING ON A BUDGET

*Budgeting is telling your money
where to go instead of asking it where it went.*

JOHN MAXWELL

*Money is a terrible master
but an excellent servant.*

P. T. BARNUM

*Economy is half the battle of life;
it is not so hard to earn money
as it is to spend it well.*

C. H. SPURGEON

*Too many people spend money
they earned to buy things they don't
want to impress people that they don't even like.*

WILL ROGERS

*Beware of little expenses.
A small leak will sink a big ship.*

BEN FRANKLIN

MONEY MANAGEMENT PRINCIPLE #4: SAVE SOMETHING FROM EVERY PAYCHECK

A recent survey conducted by BankRate.com found that just 39 percent of Americans have enough money in savings to cover an unexpected $1,000 expense. And, other studies support these findings. According to a report released by the US Federal Reserve, 44 percent of people surveyed said they could not cover an unexpected $400 emergency expense. While the details may vary from year to year and from study to study, the fact remains that, by most estimates, about 75 percent of Americans live paycheck to paycheck. No wonder so many of us are constantly stressed out about money.

Not surprisingly, a high percentage of high-income earners also manage to spend all that they make, and then some. Another survey, this one by CareerBuilder, found that almost 10 percent of the people earning $100,000 or more were living paycheck-to-paycheck. And 59 percent of the people in that high-salary range said that they were living "in the red." Clearly, we Americans have a crisis in savings, but you don't have to. You can choose to live within your means and save money from every paycheck, and that's precisely what you should do.

If you're spending everything you make today while saving nothing for tomorrow, don't be surprised if, when tomorrow comes, your bank balance approximates zero. If, however, you're serious about achieving The Good Life, you'll pare back your expenses, or get a second job, or do whatever else it takes to save money consistently. Once you form the habit of saving money each month, you won't have to endure the pressure of living paycheck-to-paycheck, at least not for long.

So, if you're already saving money from your paycheck each month, congratulations. If you have managed to build up a sensible rainy-day fund (in a savings account), double congratulations. And if you're investing the rest of your funds in sound, get-rich-slow kinds of investments (like well-managed, low-fee mutual funds), triple congratulations. If not, remember this: It's never too late to start saving for the future. And the sooner you start saving, the sooner you'll achieve financial peace of mind.

> *The habit of saving is itself an education;*
> *it fosters every virtue, teaches self-discipline,*
> *cultivates the sense of order,*
> *and broadens the mind.*
>
> T. T. MUNGER

MONEY MANAGEMENT PRINCIPLE #5: BEWARE OF HIGH-COST CONSUMER DEBT

The borrower is servant to the lender.

PROVERBS 22:7 NIV

The world that we live in has become so reliant upon debt that our entire economy depends upon it. How many new cars would dealers sell if every customer was forced to pay cash? Not very many. How many businesses would cease operations if they were forced to pay off their short-term credit lines? Plenty. And how many people would go bankrupt if they had to pay off their consumer debt by the end of the week? The answer, of course, is that millions of people would be totally underwater if they had to pay off their high-interest debt by Friday. So, let's face it: We live in a world that is addicted to debt, but you don't have to join in. Just because our society revolves around borrowed money doesn't mean that you must do likewise.

Not all debt is dangerous to your financial health. If you borrow money to purchase a well-located home—if you make a sensible down payment, and if you can comfortably afford all the expenses of owning and maintaining your residence— then you're probably making a wise decision by becoming a homeowner. Why? Because home mortgage debt, when used judiciously, can have a positive influence on your financial well-being. But other forms of debt are not so benign.

Everywhere you turn, big corporations are trying to convince you to become their debtor. Credit cards (which are advertised as "low-interest," but aren't) are easy to acquire, even easier to use, and, at times, incredibly difficult to pay off. In fact, excessive credit card debt has brought untold misery to millions of households, and it's your job to ensure that your family is spared from this needless suffering.

Sometimes, you don't even need a credit card to get yourself into trouble. Offers of "zero-down" or "zero-percent financing" are also dangerous to your financial health. When the financing looks too good to be true, it probably is. In almost every case, you're better off paying cash.

Whether you're buying a microwave, a mattress, a lawn mower, or a Maserati, somebody will probably be willing to sell it to you on credit. But the Bible makes it clear that the instant you become a debtor, you also become a servant to the lender. So the message from God's Word, updated to include the "easy-credit" world that we live in, is simply this: "Beware of consumer debt." And if you absolutely must borrow money to purchase a large item (like a car) buy a good, safe, inexpensive, used model that you can pay off in a hurry.

To sum up, debt has a few good uses and many bad

ones. So if you're trying to decide whether or not to make that next big purchase—and if you don't have enough cash in your account to pay for it—remember that when it comes to borrowed money, less is usually more. Much more.

MORE THOUGHTS ABOUT THE DANGERS OF DEBT

Debt is like any other trap. It is easy enough to get into but hard enough to get out of.

JOSH BILLINGS

Home life ceases to be free and beautiful as soon as it is founded on borrowing and debt.

HENRIK IBSEN

Pay what you owe, and you'll know what's your own.

BEN FRANKLIN

If you make a habit of spending your money before you even receive it, you will forever be wanting for something.

ST. STEPHEN OF MURET

MONEY MANAGEMENT PRINCIPLE #6: GIVE GOD HIS FAIR SHARE

One-tenth of all crops belongs to the LORD,
including the crops from fields and the fruit
from trees. That one-tenth is holy to the LORD.

LEVITICUS 27:30 NCV

In the previous chapter, we talked *generally* about generosity. Now, it's time to talk *specifically* about giving God His fair share, which, as you probably know by now, is 10%. When you stop to think about it, 10% isn't really very much. After all, the Lord has given you everything: life, love, sustenance, hope, family, and an eternal home with Him. And that's just for starters. So what does He ask in return for all those blessings? One tenth of your paycheck. No more, no less.

If you've already established the habit giving of God His fair share, you've already experienced the special blessings that the Lord bestows upon cheerful givers (like you) who honor Him with their tithes. The Lord does, indeed, love a cheerful giver. That's why generosity and joy are traveling companions. In fact, the joy of giving is woven so tightly into the fabric of the Christian faith that's almost impossible to experience The Good Life while depriving the Lord of His 10 percent.

We should never think of our tithes as gifts to God. They are, instead, a return to Him of that which is already His. God is all-powerful; He uses our offerings to accomplish His purposes, but He does not need them. We, on the other hand, desperately need the experience of tithing. And we need the assurance and peace that result from obedience to our Creator. We must tithe, first and foremost, because God has instructed us to do so. When we do, we will surely experience the abundance that accompanies a life of obedience to Him.

God doesn't need us to give Him our money.
He owns everything.
Tithing is God's way to grow Christians.

ADRIAN ROGERS

YOUR THOUGHTS ABOUT MANAGING YOUR MONEY (BEFORE IT MANAGES YOU)

In the space below, take a few moments to jot down specific steps you can take to manage your finances more prudently and, as a consequence, stop fretting about your finances. Pay attention to the ratio of your income to your expenses. And, if you need to make changes in your spending habits, be specific in the ways you can improve your financial health.

_____

_____

_____

_____

_____

_____

_____

_____

MAKE PEACE
WITH YOUR PAST

The LORD says, "Forget what happened before,
and do not think about the past. Look at the new
thing I am going to do. It is already happening.
Don't you see it? I will make a road
in the desert and rivers in the dry land."

ISAIAH 43:18–19 NCV

If you want to experience the best that life has to offer, you must make peace with your past. So, if you're harboring bitterness or regret, or anger, or hatred of any kind—if there's someone you haven't forgiven or something you haven't gotten over—the time to get over it is now. Otherwise, you may become stuck in a destructive cycle of resentment and self-pity.

Some of life's greatest roadblocks are not the ones we see through the windshield; they are, instead, the roadblocks that seem to fill the rearview mirror. Because we are imperfect beings who lack perfect control over our thoughts, we may allow ourselves to become mired in the past. Instead of focusing on the opportunities of today, we may allow painful memories to fill our minds and sap our strength. We simply can't seem to let go of our pain, so we relive it again and again, with predictably unfortunate consequences. Thankfully, God has other plans.

Philippians 3:13–14 instructs us to focus on the future, not the past: "One thing I do, forgetting those things which are behind and reaching forward to those things which are ahead, I press toward the goal for the prize of the upward call of God in Christ Jesus" (NKJV). Yet for many of us, focusing on the future is difficult indeed. Why? Part of the problem has to do with forgiveness. When we find ourselves focusing too intently on the past, it's a sure sign that we need to concentrate, instead, on a more urgent need: the need to forgive. Until we thoroughly and completely forgive those who have hurt us—and until we completely forgive ourselves—we remain stuck.

Focusing too intently on the past is fruitless and counterproductive. No amount of anger or bitterness can change what happened yesterday. Tears can't change the past; regrets can't change it. Our worries won't change the past, and neither will our complaints. Simply put, the past is, and always will be, the past. Forever.

If you've endured difficult circumstances or experienced a life-altering setback, you can appreciate how hard it can be to accept the past, entrust your future to God, and move on. But move on you must. Otherwise, you'll be stuck in an emotional prison of your own making, serving a sentence that can be commuted if—and when—you learn the art of acceptance, the wisdom of trust, and the power of forgiveness.

Can you summon both the courage and the wisdom to accept your past and move on? Can you accept the reality that yesterday—and all the yesterdays before it—are gone? And, can you entrust all those yesterdays to God? If so, you'll be blessed.

So, if you've endured a difficult past, learn from it, mourn it, memorialize it if you must, but don't live in it. Instead, build your future on a firm foundation of trust and forgiveness: trust in your heavenly Father and forgiveness for all His children, including yourself. Give all your yesterdays to God, celebrate this day, and entrust your very bright future to the Creator of the universe. The Lord intends to use you in wonderful, unexpected ways if you let Him. But first, God wants you to make peace with your past. And He wants you to do it now.

THOUGHTS ABOUT MAKING PEACE WITH YOUR PAST

We can't just put our pasts behind us.
We've got to put our pasts in front of God.

BETH MOORE

Leave the broken, irreversible past in God's hands,
and step out into the invincible future with Him.

OSWALD CHAMBERS

Don't let yesterday use up too much of today.

DENNIS SWANBERG

The wise and diligent traveler watches his every step,
and always has his eyes upon the part of the road
directly in front of him. But he does not turn constantly
backward to count every step, and to examine
every track. He would lose time in going forward.

FRANÇOIS FENELON

If you are God's child, you are no longer
bound to your past or to what you were.
You are a brand new creature in Christ Jesus.

KAY ARTHUR

FORGIVENESS NOW

Be merciful, just as your Father is merciful.

Luke 6:36 NIV

You'll never make peace with your past until you learn how to forgive all the people who have hurt you. Not just some of the people. Not just most of the people. *All* of the people. And when you forgive them, you must release the right to serve justice in your own way. Instead of seeking retribution or revenge, you must entrust justice to Christ alone.

Of course, forgiving other people can be hard—sometimes very hard. As C. S. Lewis correctly observed, "Forgiveness is a beautiful word until you have something to forgive." But God tells us that we must forgive others, even when we'd rather not. So, if you're angry with anybody (or if you're upset by something you yourself have done) the time to forgive is now.

Life would be much simpler if you could forgive people "once and for all" and be done with it. Yet forgiveness is seldom that easy. Usually, the decision to forgive is straightforward, but the process of forgiving is more difficult. Forgiveness is a journey that requires effort, time, perseverance, and prayer.

Forgiveness is a gift of great value, but ironically it's a gift that is often worth more to the giver than to the recipient. You simply cannot give the gift of forgiveness without receiving an important blessing for yourself. From a psychological perspective, the act of forgiveness relieves you of some very heavy mental baggage: persistent feelings of hatred, anger, and regret. More importantly, the act of forgiveness brings with it a spiritual blessing, a knowledge that you have honored your heavenly Father by obeying His commandments. Simply put, forgiveness is a gift that you give yourself by giving it to someone else. When you make the choice to forgive, everybody wins, especially you.

MORE THOUGHTS ABOUT FORGIVENESS

Looking back over my life, all I can see is mercy and grace written in large letters everywhere. May God help me have the same kind of heart toward those who wound or offend me.

JIM CYMBALA

If you can't seem to forgive someone, pray for that person and keep praying for him or her until, with God's help, you've removed the poison of bitterness from your heart.

MARIE T. FREEMAN

Forgiveness is God's command.

MARTIN LUTHER

Hatred is the rabid dog that turns on its owner.

MAX LUCADO

The love of God is revealed in that He laid down His life for His enemies.

OSWALD CHAMBERS

Miracles broke the physical laws of the universe;
forgiveness broke the moral rules.

PHILIP YANCEY

We are products of our past,
but we don't have to be prisoners of it.
God specializes in giving people a fresh start.

RICK WARREN

I believe that forgiveness can become
a continuing cycle: because God forgives us,
we're to forgive others; because we
forgive others, God forgives us.
Scripture presents both parts of the cycle.

SHIRLEY DOBSON

Two works of mercy set a man free:
forgive and you will be forgiven,
and give and you will receive.

ST. AUGUSTINE

God expects us to forgive others
as He has forgiven us; we are to follow
His example by having a forgiving heart.

VONETTE BRIGHT

MAKING PEACE WITH YOUR PAST

In the space below, jot down any past events, difficult people, or unfortunate circumstances that still trouble you. As you make the list, don't forget to include people you still need to forgive. And if your list is long, don't hesitate to grab an extra sheet of paper (or two!). When you've completed your list, pray about it. Ask God to give you a clean heart and a fresh start.

_____

_____

_____

_____

_____

_____

_____

_____

_____

_____

LEARN TO WORRY LESS AND TRUST GOD MORE

Do not worry about anything, but pray and ask God for everything you need, always giving thanks.

PHILIPPIANS 4:6 NCV

To experience the best that life has to offer, we must learn to worry less and to trust God more. But sometimes, especially when we face the inevitable hardships and heartbreaks that visit all of us from time to time, trusting God is hard. Perhaps that's why Jesus exhorts us to trust the Lord with a childlike faith: "I tell you the truth, you must accept the kingdom of God as if you were a child, or you will never enter it" (Luke 18:17 NCV).

Childlike trust is an attitude of belief, like the complete trust that a young child has for a parent. It's a level of trust that allows us to reach out to the Father, knowing that He will lift us up and carry us. It's the sort of faith that you've seen many times in the grocery store: a toddler reaches up toward a parent, asking to be held. That's a picture of willing dependence—saying, "I don't have strength to walk on;

please pick me up and carry me the rest of the way."

Childlike trust keeps us in relationship with the Father. We are utterly dependent on Him, and yet we're completely safe because we know that He is trustworthy. But our enemy, the devil, often challenges that trust. Neil Anderson, the founder of Freedom in Christ Ministries, wrote that "the essence of temptation is the invitation to live independently of God." When we're tempted in this way, we're being invited to make our own rules and become kings of our own little empires. We're encouraged to ignore our need for God, seeing life, instead, as a series of man-made victories. We're tempted to view ourselves as self-made men and women, claiming to be like Frank Sinatra in his signature song "My Way." On countless occasions, Sinatra sang, "I did it my way," but for those of us who seek to follow in the footsteps of God's only begotten Son, there's a superior strategy. We must do it "His way." When we do, we are blessed, and we're protected.

Sheep who wander away from the fold—the ones that wander far from the protection of the shepherd—may find excellent pasture, but they are in constant danger. The sheep that remain in the fold with the shepherd, though they may appear to be feeble and needy, are, in reality, free. In the shepherd's care, the sheep are free from unseen peril. They are free from worry. They are free to live with the quiet assurance that their protector is near and that they are always under his watchful eye. As believers, we are like the sheep that remain in the fold. We are dependent upon our Shepherd, who provides ultimate security. Whenever we depend on an all-powerful, all-knowing God, we're in very good hands!

Proverbs 29:25 teaches us that says the "fear of man will prove to be a snare, but whoever trusts in the LORD is kept safe" (NIV). And, Isaiah 26:3 promises that "You, LORD, give true peace to those who depend on you, because they trust you" (NCV). True peace sounds good, doesn't it? Childlike trust brings about true peace, the peace of mind you have when you know you're completely safe and secure in the Master's hands.

It's humbling to trust God instead of trusting in yourself. Just remember what Jesus said: whoever humbles himself like this child is the greatest in the kingdom of heaven.

This life of faith, then, consists in just this—
being a child in the Father's house.
Let the ways of childish confidence
and freedom from care, which so please
you and win your heart when you observe
your own little ones, teach you what you
should be in your attitude toward God.

HANNAH WHITALL SMITH

MORE TRUST
EQUALS LESS WORRY

Cast your burden on the LORD, and He shall sustain you; He shall never permit the righteous to be moved.

PSALM 55:22 NKJV

Even if you're a faithful believer, you may be plagued by occasional periods of anxiety or doubt. Even though you trust God's promises—even though you sincerely believe in God's love and protection—you may find yourself fretting over the countless details of everyday life. We live in a world that often breeds anxiety and fear, and when we come face to face with tough times, we may fall prey to discouragement, doubt, or depression. But our Father in heaven has other plans. God has promised that we may lead lives of abundance, not anxiety. In fact, His Word instructs us to "be anxious for nothing." But how can we put our fears to rest? By taking those fears to God and leaving them there.

Trust is an antidote to fear. So, as you face the challenges of everyday living, don't face them alone. Instead, turn every one of your concerns over to your heavenly Father in prayer. The same God who created the universe will comfort you if you ask Him...so ask Him and trust Him. Take your troubles to Him; take your fears to Him; take your doubts to Him; take your weaknesses to Him; take your sorrows to Him . . . and leave them all there. Seek protection from the One who offers you eternal salvation; build your spiritual house upon the Rock that cannot be moved.

Worry is simply thinking the same thing over and over again...and not doing anything about it.

BRANCH RICKEY

MORE THOUGHTS ABOUT WORRYING LESS AND TRUSTING GOD MORE

God is bigger than your problems.
Whatever worries press upon you today,
put them in God's hands and leave them there.

BILLY GRAHAM

How changed our lives would be
if we could only fly through the days
on wings of surrender and trust!

HANNAH WHITALL SMITH

Pray, and let God worry.

MARTIN LUTHER

We are not called to be burden-bearers,
but cross-bearers and light-bearers.
We must cast our burdens on the Lord.

CORRIE TEN BOOM

Worry is the senseless process of
cluttering up tomorrow's opportunities
with leftover problems from today.

BARBARA JOHNSON

Worry and anxiety are sand
in the machinery of life; faith is the oil.

E. STANLEY JONES

Today is mine. Tomorrow is none of my business.
If I peer anxiously into the fog of the future,
I will strain my spiritual eyes so that I will not
see clearly what is required of me now.

ELISABETH ELLIOTT

Worries carry responsibilities that
belong to God, not to you. Worry does not
enable us to escape evil; it makes us
unfit to cope with it when it comes.

CORRIE TEN BOOM

MAKE A LIST OF THINGS
YOU NEED TO TURN OVER TO GOD

In the space below, make a list of things that you've been worrying about, things that are clearly beyond your ability to control. You may want to add a few things over which you have partial, but not complete, control. When you've finished, pray about your list—and keep praying about it—while reminding yourself that God is trustworthy and that you are protected, now and forever.

_____

_____

_____

_____

_____

_____

_____

_____

_____

_____

GET ENOUGH REST AND KEEP RECHARGING YOUR BATTERY

Come to Me, all you who labor and are
heavy laden, and I will give you rest. Take My yoke
upon you and learn from Me, for I am gentle and
lowly in heart, and you will find rest for your souls.
For My yoke is easy and My burden is light.

Matthew 11:28–30 NKJV

Even the most energetic Christians can, from time to time, find themselves running on empty—and you're no exception. The demands of daily life can sap your strength, drain your energy, and rob you of the joy that is rightfully yours in Christ. When you find yourself tired, discouraged, or worse, it's time to slow down, sit down, and start recharging those spiritual batteries.

God intends that all His children (including you) lead joyous lives filled with abundance and peace. But sometimes abundance and peace seem very far away, especially when you're working on about six hours of sleep. It's hard to think clearly—or to experience joy—when you're exhausted.

Physical exhaustion is God's way of telling you to slow down, calm down, and take better care of yourself. God expects you to work hard, of course, but He also intends for you to rest. When you fail to take the rest that you need, you'll be doing a big disservice to yourself and your family.

You live in a world that tempts you to stay up late—very late. But too much late-night TV, combined with too little sleep, is a prescription for frustration, or worse.

Are your physical or spiritual batteries running low? Is your energy level flatter than a watered-down pancake? Are you too spent to smile and too tired to care? If so, it's time to turn your thoughts and your prayers to God. And when you're finished, it's probably time to turn off the lights and go to bed.

KEN REFLECTS ON THE VALUE OF VACATIONS

Like most adults trying to meet the demands of twenty-first-century life, Karen and I stay busy. Very busy. And sometimes, the demands of life at work and home can seem to go on and on without pause. There isn't a rhythm of renewal. We sleep each night and have time off every weekend, but it isn't quite enough. Thanks in part to technology, we stay connected to the to-do lists, the work, and the worries. Those short nightly or weekly reprieves don't feel nearly as exciting or life-changing as summer vacation felt when I was a kid. When that big, yellow bus lurched to a stop in front of our house on the last trip home of the school year, I leapt out with glee and didn't give school another thought for months.

As a couple, we're realizing the need to set a higher priority on routinely disconnecting and taking breaks. Not doing so can wreak havoc on our relationships, our finances, and even our health. When we try to press on through weeks or months of fatigue and work-related frustration, we eventually do things we'd resolved not to do. Instead of cooking meals from the menu we'd planned, we hurriedly pick up less healthy, more expensive take-out food. Instead of reflecting together on our day and going to sleep at a reasonable hour, we work until our brains are fried and wind down by staring at our respective screens and surfing social media or watching worthless programs. Before long, we both realize it—we need a vacation!

There isn't a rhythm of renewal. We sleep each night and have time off every weekend, but it isn't quite enough.

As financial coaches, we encourage people to make

wise money choices. When it comes to vacations, however, we don't believe the least expensive option is always the best or wisest. For example, neither of us can get excited about a "stay-cation" in which we'd stay at home for a week and do some day-trips for fun. This could save money, but it wouldn't be worth the savings. To us, vacation implies vacating the premises, as in leaving and going somewhere else for a while. If we stay at home, we simply can't disconnect from unfinished projects and other items on our mental to-do list. Even if we do nothing about them, they hang on our minds and drag us down. For the most restful break, we found that we need to go somewhere else—and of course, that costs money.

According to a report from American Express, the average vacation expense per person in the United States is $1,145, or $4,580 for a family of four. But, does a vacation have to be this expensive? We don't think so. One of my favorite childhood memories is a summer road trip to visit relatives in New England. We roamed the roads for two weeks, stopping overnight to stay with uncles, aunts, cousins, and old friends. Lodging was free. We slept on floors when needed—one night we even slept in a hayloft in my uncle's goat barn! Entertainment cost very little. We met cousins for picnics, fished with uncles, paddled canoes, and went sailing on the lakes where our uncles had modest "camps." Food was shared generously *at potluck meals. We shared messy and delicious lobster dinners, feasted on buttered corn on the cob, and licked clean our bowls of strawberry shortcake. For our family, this vagabond life was a welcome break—an experience of true refreshment and renewal.*

I've heard that, on average, Americans only use half of the vacation time for which they're eligible each year. While I can understand the economic circumstances that might motivate that self-denial, I think taking an occasional break is critical to long-term health in all areas: physical, mental, emotional, and spiritual. As hard as we work to meet our needs, there will always be more work to do. We need rest, and according to Watchman Nee, "Our rest lies in looking to the Lord, not to ourselves." Resting is an opportunity to trust God and appreciate all the blessings of life. This summer, whether you can take a vacation away from home or not, I hope you'll take time— a day or two at least—to slow down, read, pray, and enjoy family and friends. Take walks. Take naps. Notice the beauty around you. Breathe deeply. Smile. Take a break. That's what I call The Good Life!

See the world. It's more fantastic
than any dream made or paid for in factories.

RAY BRADBURY

MORE THOUGHTS ABOUT REST AND RENEWAL

*One reason so much American Christianity
is a mile wide and an inch deep is that
Christians are simply tired. Sometimes
you need to kick back and rest for Jesus's sake.*

DENNIS SWANBERG

*Satan does some of his worst work
on exhausted Christians when nerves
are frayed and their minds are faint.*

VANCE HAVNER

*Prescription for a happier and healthier life:
resolve to slow down your pace;
learn to say no gracefully; resist the temptation
to chase after more pleasure, more hobbies,
and more social entanglements.*

JAMES DOBSON

*Jesus taught us by example to get out
of the rat race and recharge our batteries.*

BARBARA JOHNSON

NOTES TO YOURSELF
ABOUT REST AND RENEWAL

In the space below, make a list of things that you can do to recharge—and keep recharging—your spiritual, physical, and emotional batteries. Include things like getting enough sleep, exercising regularly, and making time for a regular daily devotional. While you're at it, remember that it's impossible to experience The Good Life if you're too tired—or too stressed—to enjoy it.

_____

_____

_____

_____

_____

_____

_____

_____

_____

LEARN TO CONTROL YOUR THOUGHTS (BEFORE YOUR THOUGHTS CONTROL YOU)

Finally, brothers and sisters, whatever is true, whatever is noble, whatever is right, whatever is pure, whatever is lovely, whatever is admirable—if anything is excellent or praiseworthy—think about such things.

PHILIPPIANS 4:8 NIV

You cannot experience The Good Life if you're plagued by faulty thinking or chronic negativity. Negativity is highly contagious: we give it to others who, in turn, give it back to us. This cycle can be broken only by positive thoughts, heartfelt prayers, encouraging words, and meaningful acts of kindness.

Our thoughts have the power to lift us up or drag us down; they have the power to energize us or deplete us, to inspire us to greater accomplishments, or to make those accomplishments impossible. So, how will you direct your thoughts today? Will you obey the words of Philippians 4:8 by dwelling upon those things that are noble, true, and worthy of praise? Or will you allow your thoughts to be hijacked by the negativity that seems to dominate our troubled world?

The Lord intends that you experience joy and abundance, but He will not force His joy upon you; you must claim it for yourself. It's up to you to celebrate the life that God has given you by focusing your mind upon "whatever is admirable." Today, try to spend more time thinking about your blessings, and less time fretting about your hardships. Then, take time to thank the Giver of all things good for gifts that are, in truth, far too numerous to count.

As thoughtful servants of a loving God, we have no valid reason—and no legitimate excuse—to be negative. So, when we are tempted to be overly critical of others, or unfairly critical of ourselves, we must use the transforming power of God's love to break the chains of negativity. We must defeat negativity before negativity defeats us. It's the proper way to think and the only way to fully experience The Good Life.

REDIRECTING YOUR THOUGHTS

Our thoughts have the power to shape our lives—for better or worse. Thoughts have the power to lift our spirits, to improve our circumstances, and to strengthen our relationship with the Creator. But, our thoughts also have the power to cause us great harm if we focus too intently upon those things that distance us from God.

Sometimes, if we're not careful, we can be victimized by runaway thoughts. The process may start innocently enough, with a small, negative emotional spark that ignites an inferno of negative consequences. The challenge, of course, is to correct and corral inappropriate thoughts *before* they stampede through the landscape of our lives, not after.

Do you pay careful attention to the quality and direction of your thoughts? And are you careful to direct those thoughts toward topics that are uplifting, enlightening, and pleasing to God? If so, congratulations. But if you find that your emotions are being hijacked from time to time by the negativity that seems to have invaded our troubled world, it's time to start thinking constructively about the quality and the direction of your thoughts.

Today and every day, make your thoughts an offering to God. Seek—by the things you think and the actions you take—to honor Him and serve Him. He deserves no less. And neither, for that matter, do you.

The secret of living a life of excellence is merely a matter of thinking thoughts of excellence. Really, it's a matter of programming our minds with the kind of information that will set us free.

CHARLES SWINDOLL

THE IMPORTANCE OF CHILDLIKE HOPE

But we are hoping for something we do not have yet,
and we are waiting for it patiently.

ROMANS 8:25 NCV

Most children are, by nature, hopeful. Childlike hope is characterized by wide-eyed optimism, not gloomy pessimism. It's the belief that something good might be just around the corner. It's looking at roses, not thorns, and at silver linings, not clouds. It's the ability to have faith in the future without a trace of cynicism or doubt.

In a book called *Please Don't Squeeze the Christian*, author Scott Sernau reflects on the danger of cynicism—especially in the life of believers who claim a "living hope." He writes: "Cynicism kills in the manner of frostbite: the only symptom is a deadening numbness. And even Christians are often tinged with this frostbite. Callousness and doubt numb us to life and joy.... Doubt can be a state of mind—or it can be a way of life."

Childlike hope counters that doubt. But because we live in troubling times, we're constantly bombarded by cynical messages delivered by pessimistic messengers. So it's no surprise that our thoughts can be hijacked by negative messages that feed our fears and attack our faith.

Hope is a scriptural cure for pessimism, and we can find it in Romans. It's a prayer that we can pray as often as we like, and it never grows old. Here's what it says:

May the God of hope fill you with all joy and peace as you trust in him, so that you may overflow with hope by the power of the Holy Spirit.

ROMANS 15:13 NIV

This beautiful prayer encourages us trust God with childlike hope. It's a lesson we must never forget.

MORE THOUGHTS ON HOPE

Oh, remember this: There is never a time when we may not hope in God. Whatever our necessities, however great our difficulties, and though to all appearance help is impossible, yet our business is to hope in God, and it will be found that it is not in vain.

GEORGE MUELLER

Love is the seed of all hope. It is the enticement to trust, to risk, to try, and to go on.

GLORIA GAITHER

I wish I could make it all new again; I can't. But God can. "He restores my soul," wrote the shepherd. God doesn't reform; He restores. He doesn't camouflage the old; He restores the new. The Master Builder will pull out the original plan and restore it. He will restore the vigor, He will restore the energy. He will restore the hope. He will restore the soul.

MAX LUCADO

Faith looks back and draws courage; hope looks ahead and keeps desire alive.

JOHN ELDREDGE

I discovered that sorrow was not to be feared but rather endured with hope and expectancy that God would use it to visit and bless my life.

JILL BRISCOE

The hope we have in Jesus is the anchor for the soul—something sure and steadfast, preventing drifting or giving way, lowered to the depth of God's love.

FRANKLIN GRAHAM

Nothing worth doing is completed in our lifetimes, therefore we must be saved by hope.

REINHOLD NIEBUHR

BE OPTIMISTIC

Make me hear joy and gladness.

PSALM 51:8 NKJV

Pessimism and Christianity don't mix. Why? Because Christians have every reason to be optimistic about life here on earth and life eternal. As C. H. Spurgeon observed, "Our hope in Christ for the future is the mainstream of our joy." But sometimes we fall prey to worry, frustration, anxiety, or sheer exhaustion, and our hearts become heavy. What's needed is plenty of rest, a large dose of perspective, and God's healing touch, but not necessarily in that order.

Today, make this promise to yourself and keep it: vow to be a hope-filled Christian. Think realistically and optimistically about your life, your profession, and your future. Trust your hopes, not your fears. Take time to celebrate God's glorious creation. And then, when you've filled your heart with hope and gladness, share your optimism with others. They'll be better for it, and so will you. But not necessarily in that order.

MAKE A LIST OF NEGATIVE THOUGHTS THAT NEED TO BE REDIRECTED

In the space below, jot down any exaggerated, negative, repetitive thoughts that have been bothering you lately. Then, take time to look realistically at the things that have been troubling you. Are they really as bad as you've made them out to be? If so, take action. If not, make a practice of catching those negative thoughts before they run away with your emotions.

_____

_____

_____

_____

_____

_____

_____

_____

_____

EXPERIENCING THE GOOD LIFE IN EVERY SEASON

I have learned to be content
whatever the circumstances.

PHILIPPIANS 4:11 NIV

Life doesn't stand still for any of us. To the contrary, the journey from cradle to grave is an adventure in change: our circumstances change; our bodies age; and, the world around us changes, too. When times are good and life seems to be proceeding as planned, it's easier to be contented. But when we're confronted with unwelcome changes, we're tempted to moan, to groan, to complain, and to do little else. But if we are to enjoy The Good Life, we must learn to be contented in every stage of life. Like Paul in his letter to the Philippians, we must learn to be content, whatever our circumstances.

Our world is in a state of constant change. God is not. At times, the world seems to be trembling beneath our feet. But we can be comforted in the knowledge that our heavenly Father is the rock that cannot be shaken. His Word promises, "I am the LORD, I do not change" (Malachi 3:6 NKJV).

Every day that we live, we mortals encounter a multitude of changes—some good, some not so good. And on occasion, all of us must endure life-changing personal losses that leave us heartbroken. When we do, our heavenly Father stands ready to comfort us, to guide us, and—in time—to heal us.

Is the world spinning a little too fast for your liking? Are you facing difficult circumstances or unwelcome changes? If so, please remember that God is far bigger than any problem you may face. So, instead of worrying about life's inevitable challenges, put your faith in the Father and His only begotten Son. After all, "Jesus Christ is the same yesterday, today, and forever" (Hebrews 13:8 NKJV). And it is precisely because your Savior does not change that you can face your challenges with courage for today and hope for tomorrow. The Creator of the universe will protect you if you ask Him . . . so ask Him . . . and then serve Him with willing hands and a trusting heart.

There is a time for everything, and a season
for every activity under heaven.

ECCLESIASTES 3:1 NIV

*Great relief and satisfaction can come from seeking
God's priorities for us in each season, discerning what
is "best" in the midst of many noble opportunities, and
pouring our most excellent energies into those things.*

BETH MOORE

FREEDOM FROM WORRIES ABOUT THE FUTURE

But seek first his kingdom and his righteousness, and all these things will be given to you as well. Therefore do not worry about tomorrow, for tomorrow will worry about itself. Each day has enough trouble of its own.

MATTHEW 6:33–34 NIV

Sometimes the future seems bright, and sometimes it does not. Yet even when we cannot see the possibilities of tomorrow, God can. Our challenge is to trust ourselves to do the best work we can, and then to trust God to do the rest.

When we trust God, we should trust Him without reservation. We should steel ourselves against the inevitable disappointments of the day, secure in the knowledge that our heavenly Father has a plan for the future that is brighter than we can imagine.

Are you willing to look to the future with trust and confidence? Hopefully so, because the future should not be feared, it should be embraced. And it most certainly should be embraced *by you.*

The Christian believes in a fabulous future.

BILLY GRAHAM

MORE THOUGHTS ABOUT YOUR VERY BRIGHT FUTURE

Do not limit the limitless God! With Him, face the future unafraid because you are never alone.

MRS. CHARLES E. COWMAN

Take courage. We walk in the wilderness today and in the Promised Land tomorrow.

D. L. MOODY

No matter how heavy the burden, daily strength is given, so I expect we need not give ourselves any concern as to what the outcome will be. We must simply go forward.

ANNIE ARMSTRONG

The past is our teacher; the present is our opportunity; the future is our friend.

EDWIN LOUIS COLE

Never be afraid to trust an unknown future to a known God.

CORRIE TEN BOOM

PLANNING YOUR
VERY BRIGHT FUTURE

In the space below, jot down future events that you're excited about. Don't restrict yourself to earthly victories (like a promotion at work or the birth of a grandchild). Also, be sure to make note of God's amazing gift to you: the gift of eternal life through His Son, Jesus.

_____

_____

_____

_____

_____

_____

_____

_____

_____

_____

PUT GOD IN HIS RIGHTFUL PLACE: FIRST PLACE

You shall have no other gods before Me.

EXODUS 20:3 NKJV

The final step in claiming The Good Life—and the most important step of all—has to do with a relationship: the relationship you establish with your Father in heaven and His only begotten Son. Christ sacrificed His life on the cross so that we might have eternal life. This gift, freely given, is the priceless possession of everyone who accepts Him as Lord and Savior.

It is by God's grace that we have been saved, through faith. We are saved not because of our good deeds but because of our faith in Christ. May we, who have been given so much, praise our Savior for the gift of salvation, and may we share the joyous news of our Master's love and His grace.

As you contemplate your own relationship with God, remember this: all of mankind is engaged in the practice of worship. Some people choose to worship God and, as a result, reap the joy that He intends for His children. Others distance themselves from God by worshiping such things as earthly possessions or personal gratification...and when they do so, they suffer.

In the book of Exodus, God warns that we should place no gods before Him. Yet all too often, we place our Lord in second, third, or fourth place as we worship the gods of pride, greed, power, fame, or personal gratification. When we place our desires for material possessions above our love for God—or when we yield to any other worldly temptation—we find ourselves engaged in a struggle that is similar to the one Jesus faced when He was tempted by Satan. In the wilderness, Satan offered Jesus earthly power and unimaginable riches, but Jesus turned Satan away and chose instead to worship God. We must do likewise by putting God first and worshiping only Him.

Does God rule your heart? Make certain that the honest answer to this question is a resounding yes. In the life of every righteous believer, God comes first. And that's precisely the place that He deserves in your heart, too.

Jesus Christ is the first and last, author and finisher, beginning and end, alpha and omega, and by Him all other things hold together. He must be first or nothing. God never comes next!

VANCE HAVNER

MORE THOUGHTS ABOUT PUTTING GOD FIRST

*Anything that makes religion a second object
makes it no object. He who offers to God
a second place offers Him no place.*

JOHN RUSKIN

*There is no way that we can be effective disciples
of Christ except through relentless pruning—
the cutting away of non-fruitbearing suckers
that sap our energies, but bear no fruit.*

SELWYN HUGHES

*Jesus challenges you and me to keep our focus daily
on the cross of His will if we want to be His disciples.*

ANNE GRAHAM LOTZ

*You must never sacrifice your relationship with God
for the sake of a relationship with another person.*

CHARLES STANLEY

*Make God's will the focus of your life day by day.
If you seek to please Him and Him alone,
you'll find yourself satisfied with life.*

KAY ARTHUR

KEN'S REFLECTIONS ON KNOWING GOD'S WILL AND MAKING A DIFFERENCE

How can I know God's will for my life? And how do I live it out? Trying harder isn't the key. No, the first thing I need to realize is that the path God has planned for me will only be possible through the work of Jesus Christ in my life. I cannot, even with my best efforts, be the kind of man God wants me to be without Jesus.

Instead, I have to walk out the verse that has become my favorite verse—my life verse: Galatians 2:20: "I have been crucified with Christ and I no longer live, but Christ lives in me. The life I now live in the body, I live by faith in the Son of God, who loved me and gave himself for me" (NIV).

With Christ in me, I have power, motivation, and direction. I know God's will for my life. I may not know the details of His plan ahead of time, but I know what He wants me to do today. It's not a mystery—it's right there in the Word of God. Here are a few examples, a few verses that would create a legacy with my life if I lived them out every day as empowered by Christ who lives in me:

Be kind and compassionate to one another, forgiving each other, just as in Christ God forgave you. (Ephesians 4:32)

Follow God's example, therefore, as dearly loved children and walk in the way of love, just as Christ loved us and gave himself up for us as a fragrant offering and sacrifice to God. (Ephesians 5:1–2)

And whatever you do, whether in word or deed, do it all in the name of the Lord Jesus, giving thanks to God the Father through him. (Colossians 3:17)

Make the most of every opportunity. (Colossians 4:5)

Set your minds on things above, not on earthly things. (Colossians 3:2)

Devote yourselves to prayer, being watchful and thankful. (Colossians 4:2)

Rejoice always, pray continually, give thanks in all circumstances; for this is God's will for you in Christ Jesus. (1 Thessalonians 5:16–18)

These are but a handful of verses that give meaning to my day. The Word is filled with guidance about how to live a life that honors the Lord and makes a difference in the lives of other people.

CHARLES T. STUDD: ONLY ONE LIFE

Each of us has but one life to live. And since none of us know precisely when that life will end, we should strive to do God's will every day, with no exceptions. One person who did God's will, a man who was a true hero of the Christian faith, was a nineteenth-century missionary named C. T. Studd. We conclude with his story and his most memorable poem:

Charles T. Studd (1860–1931) was a nineteenth-century pioneering missionary to China, India, and Africa. This man was a true servant of the Lord. He is remembered, according to one historical account, for "his courage in any emergency, his determination never to sound the retreat, his conviction that he was in God's will, his faith that God would see him through, his contempt of the arm of the flesh, and his willingness to risk all for Christ." C. T. Studd was a quite a guy.

Studd was born in England in 1860 into a Christian family. He was one of three sons of a wealthy retired planter, Edward Studd, who had made a fortune in India and had come back to England to spend it. While in England, Edward encountered D. L. Moody, the nineteenth-century evangelist, who was preaching in evangelistic campaigns. It was at one of these meetings that Edward Studd (C. T.'s father) became a Christian. C. T. was seventeen when his father came to Christ.

C. T. was saved in 1878 at the age of eighteen when a preacher, upon visiting their home, asked C. T. an uncomfortable question: "Are you a Christian?" C. T. gave an unconvincing answer, so the preacher kept up the conversation, talking about how grateful God's children should be that God would be willing to give them the gift of eternal life. At the end of the conversation, C. T. recounted, "I got down on my knees and I did say 'thank You' to God. And right then and there joy and peace came into my soul. I knew then what it was to be 'born again,' and the Bible which had been so dry to me before, became everything."

C. T.'s two brothers were also saved that same day!

During C. T.'s lifetime, he took part in Hudson Taylor's outreach in China. In his mid-twenties, while serving in China, C. T. inherited his fortune from his father's estate and gave it away to fund D. L. Moody's evangelistic work, George Muller's work with orphans, and other missionary causes. His family and friends back home thought he was foolish to do this, but one biographer wrote that "this was not a fool's plunge on his part. It was his public testimony before God and man that he believed God's Word to be the surest thing on earth, and that the hundred-fold interest which God has promised in this life, not to speak of the next, is an actual reality for those who believe it and act on it."

One writer observed, "C. T.'s life stands as some rugged Gibraltar—a sign to all succeeding generations that it is worthwhile to lose all this world can offer and stake everything on the world to come. His life will be an eternal rebuke to easy going Christianity. He has demonstrated what it means to follow Christ without counting the cost and without looking back."

One part of his legacy is well known to this day; perhaps you've heard of it. It's a poem he wrote called "Only One Life." The most familiar line from the poem is "Only one life, 'twill soon be past, Only what's done for Christ will last." But the entire poem is noteworthy, so we've chosen it as fitting conclusion to *The Good Life*.

ONLY ONE LIFE

By C. T. Studd

Two little lines I heard one day,
Traveling along life's busy way;
Bringing conviction to my heart,
And from my mind would not depart;
Only one life, 'twill soon be past,
Only what's done for Christ will last.

Only one life, yes only one,
Soon will its fleeting hours be done;
Then, in "that day" my Lord to meet,
And stand before His Judgment seat;
Only one life, 'twill soon be past,
Only what's done for Christ will last.

Only one life, the still small voice,
Gently pleads for a better choice
Bidding me selfish aims to leave,
And to God's holy will to cleave;
Only one life, 'twill soon be past,
Only what's done for Christ will last.

Only one life, a few brief years,
Each with its burdens, hopes, and fears;
Each with its days I must fulfill,
Living for self or in His will;
Only one life, 'twill soon be past,
Only what's done for Christ will last.

When this bright world would tempt me sore,
When Satan would a victory score;
When self would seek to have its way,
Then help me Lord with joy to say;
Only one life, 'twill soon be past,
Only what's done for Christ will last.

Give me, Father, a purpose deep,
In joy or sorrow Thy word to keep;
Faithful and true what 'er the strife,
Pleasing Thee in my daily life;
Only one life, 'twill soon be past,
Only what's done for Christ will last.

Oh let my love with fervor burn,
And from the world now let me turn;
Living for Thee, and Thee alone,
Bringing Thee pleasure on Thy throne;
Only one life, 'twill soon be past,
Only what's done for Christ will last.

Only one life, yes only one,
Now let me say, "Thy will be done";
And when at last I'll hear the call,
I know I'll say, "'Twas worth it all";
Only one life, 'twill soon be past,
Only what's done for Christ will last.

WHAT WILL YOU DO
WITH YOUR ONE LIFE?

In the space below, jot down a short personal mission statement. Try to keep it brief, making note of only the goals and values that are most important to you. And as you're writing, remember the words of C. T. Studd: "Only what's done for Christ will last."

_____

_____

_____

_____

_____

_____

_____

_____

_____

_____

VERSES AND QUOTES ABOUT LIVING THE GOOD LIFE NOW

Arranged Alphabetically by Topic

Throughout this book, we've included numerous quotations and Bible verses. In this section, we've arranged some of our favorite verses and quotes by topic. We hope that the promises and principles that are summarized on the following pages will serve as timely reminders that you can live The Good Life, starting today. And that's precisely what you should do.

TOPICS

Abundance

Acceptance

Accepting Christ

Action

Adversity

Anxiety and Worry

Asking God

Attitude

New Beginnings

Bible Study

Blessings

Celebration

Change

Cheerfulness

Christ's Love

Confidence

Conscience	Focus
Decisions	Following Christ
Disappointments	Forgiveness
Discipleship	Friends and Friendship
Discipline	Future
Discouragement	God First
Distractions	God's Guidance
Dreams	God's Plan
Encouragement	God's Promises
Enthusiasm	God's Support
Eternal Life, Eternity	God's Timing
Example	Gratitude
Excellence	Habits
Excuses	Happiness
Failure	Hope
Faith	Humility
Family	Integrity
Fear	Jesus
Fellowship	Joy

ABUNDANCE

I have come that they may have life,
and that they may have it more abundantly.

John 10:10 NKJV

*The man who lives without Jesus is the poorest
of the poor, whereas no one is so rich
as the man who lives in His grace.*

Thomas à Kempis

*God is sufficient for all our needs,
for every problem, for every difficulty,
for every broken heart, for every human sorrow.*

Peter Marshall

*God loves you and wants you to experience
peace and life—abundant and eternal.*

Billy Graham

*Ask, and it will be given to you; seek, and you
will find; knock, and it will be opened to you.
For everyone who asks receives, and he who seeks
finds, and to him who knocks it will be opened.*

Matthew 7:7–8 NKJV

ACCEPTANCE

Should we accept only good
from God and not adversity?

Job 2:10 HCSB

Subdue your heart to match your circumstances.

Joni Eareckson Tada

*Acceptance says, "True, this is my situation at the
moment. I'll look unblinkingly at the reality of it.
But, I'll also open my hands to accept willingly
whatever a loving Father sends."*

Catherine Marshall

*One of the marks of spiritual maturity is the quiet
confidence that God is in control, without the need
to understand why He does what He does.*

Charles Swindoll

*Christians who are strong in the faith grow as they
accept whatever God allows to enter their lives.*

Billy Graham

I have learned in whatever state I am, to be content.

Philippians 4:11 NKJV

ACCEPTING CHRIST

If you confess with your mouth, "Jesus is Lord,"
and believe in your heart that God raised him from
the dead, you will be saved. For it is with your heart
that you believe and are justified, and it is with
your mouth that you confess and are saved.

Romans 10:9–10 NIV

*Ultimately, our relationship with Christ
is the one thing we cannot do without.*

Beth Moore

*Christ is the horn of our salvation, the One
who was secured on a cross so that we could
be secured in the Lamb's book of Life.*

Beth Moore

And he said to them: "I tell you the truth,
unless you change and become like little children,
you will never enter the kingdom of heaven.
Therefore, whoever humbles himself like
this child is the greatest in heaven."

Matthew 18:3–4 NIV

ACTION

Therefore, get your minds ready for action,
being self-disciplined, and set your hope
completely on the grace to be brought
to you at the revelation of Jesus Christ.

1 PETER 1:13 HCSB

*Pray as though everything depended on God.
Work as though everything depended on you.*

ST. AUGUSTINE

Authentic faith cannot help but act.

BETH MOORE

*Do noble things, not dream them all day long;
and so make life, death, and that vast forever
one grand, sweet song.*

CHARLES KINGSLEY

But be doers of the word,
and not hearers only, deceiving yourselves.

JAMES 1:22 NKJV

ADVERSITY

God blesses the people who patiently endure testing.
Afterward they will receive the crown of life that God
has promised to those who love him.

JAMES 1:12 NLT

*Human problems are never greater
than divine solutions.*

ERWIN LUTZER

*Often God has to shut a door in our face
so that He can subsequently open the door
through which He wants us to go.*

CATHERINE MARSHALL

*God is in control. He may not take away
trials or make detours for us,
but He strengthens us through them.*

BILLY GRAHAM

*For whatever is born of God
overcomes the world. And this is the victory
that has overcome the world—our faith.*

1 JOHN 5:4 NKJV

ANXIETY AND WORRY

Let not your heart be troubled; you believe in God,
believe also in Me.

John 14:1 NKJV

*Worry is the senseless process of cluttering
up tomorrow's opportunities with
leftover problems from today.*

Barbara Johnson

*Look around you and you'll be distressed;
look within yourself and you'll be depressed;
look at Jesus, and you'll be at rest!*

Corrie ten Boom

*Knowing that God is faithful really helps me
to not be captivated by worry.*

Josh McDowell

Therefore do not worry about tomorrow,
for tomorrow will worry about itself.
Each day has enough trouble of its own.

Matthew 6:34 NIV

ASKING GOD

Ask, and it will be given to you; seek, and you will find; knock, and it will be opened to you. For everyone who asks receives, and he who seeks finds, and to him who knocks it will be opened.

MATTHEW 7:7-8 NKJV

God will help us become the people
we are meant to be, if only we will ask Him.

HANNAH WHITALL SMITH

You pay God a compliment
by asking great things of Him.

ST. TERESA OF AVILA

When you ask God to do something,
don't ask timidly; put your whole heart into it.

MARIE T. FREEMAN

You did not choose Me, but I chose you. I appointed you that you should go out and produce fruit, and that your fruit should remain, so that whatever you ask the Father in My name, He will give you.

JOHN 15:16 HCSB

ATTITUDE

Make your own attitude that of Christ Jesus.

PHILIPPIANS 2:5 HCSB

We choose what attitudes we have right now.
And it's a continuing choice.

JOHN MAXWELL

Your attitude, not your aptitude,
will determine your altitude.

ZIG ZIGLAR

The things we think are the things that feed our souls.
If we think on pure and lovely things,
we shall grow pure and lovely like them;
and the converse is equally true.

HANNAH WHITALL SMITH

Finally, brethren, whatever is true,
whatever is honorable, whatever is right,
whatever is pure, whatever is lovely, whatever is
of good repute, if there is any excellence and if
anything worthy of praise, dwell on these things.

PHILIPPIANS 4:8 NASB

NEW BEGINNINGS

Do not remember the past events,
pay no attention to things of old. Look,
I am about to do something new; even now
it is coming. Do you not see it? Indeed, I will make
a way in the wilderness, rivers in the desert.

ISAIAH 43:18–19 HCSB

God specializes in giving people a fresh start.

RICK WARREN

Each day you must say to yourself,
"Today I am going to begin."

JEAN PIERRE DE CAUSSADE

There is wonderful freedom and joy in coming
to recognize that the fun is in the becoming.

GLORIA GAITHER

You are being renewed in the spirit of your minds;
you put on the new man, the one created according
to God's likeness in righteousness and purity of the truth.

EPHESIANS 4:23–24 HCSB

BIBLE STUDY

But grow in the grace and knowledge
of our Lord and Savior Jesus Christ.
To Him be the glory both now and forever. Amen.

2 PETER 3:18 NKJV

*Gather the riches of God's promises.
Nobody can take away from you those texts
from the Bible which you have learned by heart.*

CORRIE TEN BOOM

*Read the scripture, not only as history,
but as a love letter sent to you from God.*

THOMAS WATSON

*If we neglect the Bible, we cannot expect
to benefit from the wisdom and direction
that result from knowing God's Word.*

VONETTE BRIGHT

The counsel of the LORD stands forever,
the plans of His heart to all generations.

PSALM 33:11 NKJV

BLESSINGS

For You, Lord, bless the righteous one;
You surround him with favor like a shield.

Psalm 5:12 HCSB

*God is the giver, and we are the receivers.
And His richest gifts are bestowed not upon
those who do the greatest things, but upon those
who accept His abundance and His grace.*

Hannah Whitall Smith

*God is always trying to give good things to us,
but our hands are too full to receive them.*

St. Augustine

*It is God's will to bless us, but not necessarily
on our terms. Sometimes what we think would be
a wonderful blessing would not bless us at all.*

Joyce Meyer

For the Lord is good; His mercy is everlasting,
and His truth endures to all generations.

Psalm 100:5 NKJV

CELEBRATION

This is the day the LORD has made;
we will rejoice and be glad in it.

PSALM 118:24 NKJV

Every day we live is a priceless gift of God,
loaded with possibilities to learn something new,
to gain fresh insights.

DALE EVANS ROGERS

There is not one blade of grass,
there is no color in this world
that is not intended to make us rejoice.

JOHN CALVIN

All our life is celebration to us.
We are convinced, in fact,
that God is always everywhere.

ST. CLEMENT OF ALEXANDRIA

Rejoice in the Lord always.
I will say it again: Rejoice!

PHILIPPIANS 4:4 NIV

CHANGE

To everything there is a season,
a time for every purpose under heaven.

ECCLESIASTES 3:1 NKJV

Are you on the eve of change? Embrace it.
Accept it. Don't resist it. Change is not only
a part of life, change is a necessary part
of God's strategy. To use us to change
the world, He alters our assignments.

MAX LUCADO

Change always starts in your mind.
The way you think determines the way you feel,
and the way you feel influences the way you act.

RICK WARREN

The world changes—circumstances change,
we change—but God's Word never changes.

WARREN WIERSBE

The wise see danger ahead and avoid it,
but fools keep going and get into trouble.

PROVERBS 22:3 NCV

CHEERFULNESS

For the happy heart, life is a continual feast.

PROVERBS 15:15 NLT

*The practical effect of Christianity
is happiness, therefore let it be spread
abroad everywhere!*

C. H. SPURGEON

*The greatest honor you can give
Almighty God is to live gladly and joyfully
because of the knowledge of His love.*

JULIANA OF NORWICH

*Focus on giving smiles away
and you will always discover that your
own smiles will always be in great supply!*

JOYCE MEYER

Rejoice always! Pray constantly.
Give thanks in everything,
for this is God's will for you in Christ Jesus.

1 THESSALONIANS 5:16–18 HCSB

CHRIST'S LOVE

I am the good shepherd.
The good shepherd gives His life for the sheep.

John 10:11 NKJV

Jesus is all compassion.
He never betrays us.

Catherine Marshall

Jesus: the proof of God's love.

Phillip Yancey

As the love of a husband for his bride,
such is the love of Christ for His people.

C. H. Spurgeon

Christ has turned all our sunsets into dawns.

St. Clement of Alexandria

If anyone belongs to Christ,
there is a new creation.
The old things have gone;
everything is made new!

2 Corinthians 5:17 NCV

CONFIDENCE

That is why we can say with confidence,
"The Lord is my helper, so I will not be afraid.
What can mere mortals do to me?"

HEBREWS 13:6 NLT

*We never get anywhere—nor do our
conditions and circumstances change—
when we look at the dark side of life.*

LETTIE COWMAN

*You need to make the right decision—
firmly and decisively—and then stick with it,
with God's help.*

BILLY GRAHAM

*God's all-sufficiency is a major. Your inability
is a minor. Major in majors, not in minors.*

CORRIE TEN BOOM

I have told you these things so that in Me you
may have peace. In the world you have suffering.
But take courage! I have conquered the world.

JOHN 16:33 HCSB

CONSCIENCE

I always do my best to have a clear
conscience toward God and men.

Acts 24:16 HCSB

*Conscience is our wisest counselor and teacher,
our most faithful and most patient friend.*

BILLY GRAHAM

*God desires that we become spiritually healthy
enough through faith to have a conscience that
rightly interprets the work of the Holy Spirit.*

BETH MOORE

A sense of deity is inscribed on every heart.

JOHN CALVIN

Conscience can only be satisfied if God is satisfied.

C. H. SPURGEON

Let us draw near to God with a sincere heart
in full assurance of faith, having our hearts
sprinkled to cleanse us from a guilty conscience
and having our bodies washed with pure water.

HEBREWS 10:22 NIV

DECISIONS

He will teach us His ways,
and we shall walk in His paths.

ISAIAH 2:3 NKJV

A man who honors God privately will show it
by making good decisions publicly.

EDWIN LOUIS COLE

Every day, I find countless opportunities to decide
whether I will obey God and demonstrate my love
for Him or try to please myself or the world system.
God is waiting for my choices.

BILL BRIGHT

Your choices and decisions are a reflection
of how well you've set and followed your priorities.

ELIZABETH GEORGE

If any of you lacks wisdom,
he should ask God, who gives
generously to all without finding fault,
and it will be given to him.

JAMES 1:5 NIV

DISAPPOINTMENTS

Give your burdens to the Lord,
and he will take care of you.
He will not permit the godly to slip and fall.

Psalm 55:22 NLT

*We all have sorrows and disappointments,
but one must never forget that, if commended
to God, they will issue in good. His own solution
is far better than any we could conceive.*

Fanny Crosby

*If your hopes are being disappointed just now,
it means that they are being purified.*

Oswald Chambers

*Allow God to use the difficulties
and disappointments in life as polish
to transform your faith into a glistening diamond
that takes in and reflects His love.*

Elizabeth George

God shall wipe away all the tears from their eyes.

Revelation 7:17 KJV

DISCIPLESHIP

Whosoever will come after me, let him deny himself,
and take up his cross, and follow me.

MARK 8:34 KJV

*Our Lord's conception of discipleship is not that
we work for God, but that God works through us.*

OSWALD CHAMBERS

*Jesus challenges you and me to keep our focus daily
on the cross of His will if we want to be His disciples.*

ANNE GRAHAM LOTZ

*A disciple is a follower of Christ. That means you take
on His priorities as your own. His agenda becomes
your agenda. His mission becomes your mission.*

CHARLES STANLEY

*Discipleship usually brings us into the necessity
of choice between duty and desire.*

ELISABETH ELLIOT

For whoever does the will of My Father in heaven,
that person is My brother and sister and mother.

MATTHEW 12:50 HCSB

DISCIPLINE

So prepare your minds for action and exercise
self-control. Put all your hope in the
gracious salvation that will come to you
when Jesus Christ is revealed to the world.

1 PETER 1:13 NLT

*Forgiveness does not change the past,
but it does enlarge the future.*

DAVID JEREMIAH

*Forgiveness is an act of the will,
and the will can function regardless
of the temperature of the heart.*

CORRIE TEN BOOM

Forgiveness is God's command.

MARTIN LUTHER

Work hard, but not just to please your masters
when they are watching. As slaves of Christ,
do the will of God with all your heart.
Work with enthusiasm, as though you were
working for the Lord rather than for people.

EPHESIANS 6:6–7 NLT

DISCOURAGEMENT

But as for you, be strong; don't be discouraged,
for your work has a reward.

2 CHRONICLES 15:7 HCSB

*If your hopes are being disappointed just now,
it means that they are being purified.*

OSWALD CHAMBERS

*Feelings of uselessness and hopelessness
are not from God, but from the evil one,
the devil, who wants to discourage you
and thwart your effectiveness for the Lord.*

BILL BRIGHT

*Look around you and you'll be distressed;
look within yourself and you'll be depressed;
look at Jesus, and you'll be at rest!*

CORRIE TEN BOOM

Let not your heart be troubled;
you believe in God, believe also in Me.

JOHN 14:1 NKJV

DISTRACTIONS

Let us throw off everything that hinders
and the sin that so easily entangles, and let us run
with perseverance the race marked out for us.

HEBREWS 12:1 NIV

*The whole point of getting things done
is knowing what to leave undone.*

OSWALD CHAMBERS

*You cannot overestimate the unimportance
of practically everything.*

JOHN MAXWELL

*There is nothing quite as potent
as a focused life, one lived on purpose.*

RICK WARREN

But this one thing I do, forgetting those things
which are behind, and reaching forth
unto those things which are before,
I press toward the mark for the prize
of the high calling of God in Christ Jesus.

PHILIPPIANS 3:13–14 KJV

DREAMS

A dream fulfilled is a tree of life.

PROVERBS 13:12 NLT

When the dream of our heart
is one that God has planted there,
a strange happiness flows into us.
At that moment, the spiritual resources
of the universe are released to help us.

CATHERINE MARSHALL

God's gifts put men's best dreams to shame.

ELIZABETH BARRETT BROWNING

Two types of voices command your attention today.
Negative ones fill your mind with doubt, bitterness,
and fear. Positive ones purvey hope and strength.
Which one will you choose to heed?

MAX LUCADO

But we are hoping for something
we do not have yet, and we are
waiting for it patiently.

ROMANS 8:25 NCV

ENCOURAGEMENT

But encourage each other daily,
while it is still called today, so that none of you
is hardened by sin's deception.

HEBREWS 3:13 HCSB

Developing a positive attitude
means working continually to find
what is uplifting and encouraging.

BARBARA JOHNSON

Don't forget that a single sentence,
spoken at the right moment,
can change somebody's whole perspective on life.
A little encouragement can go a long, long way.

MARIE T. FREEMAN

When we are the comfort and encouragement
to others, we are sometimes surprised
at how it comes back to us many times over.

BILLY GRAHAM

Bear one another's burdens,
and so fulfill the law of Christ.

GALATIANS 6:2 NKJV

ENTHUSIASM

Whatever you do, do it enthusiastically,
as something done for the Lord and not for men.

Colossians 3:23 HCSB

*Wherever you are, be all there. Live to the hilt
every situation you believe to be the will of God.*

Jim Elliot

*Those who have achieved excellence
in the practice of an art or profession
have commonly been motivated
by great enthusiasm in their pursuit of it.*

John Knox

*Consider each day, as it were,
a beginning, and always act with
the same fervour as on the first day you began.*

St. Anthony of Padua

Rejoice always! Pray constantly.
Give thanks in everything,
for this is God's will for you in Christ Jesus.

1 Thessalonians 5:16–18 HCSB

ETERNAL LIFE, ETERNITY

For God so loved the world,
that he gave his only begotten Son,
that whosoever believeth in him should not perish,
but have everlasting life.

JOHN 3:16 KJV

Death is not the end of life;
it is only the gateway to eternity.

BILLY GRAHAM

Everything that is joined to the immortal Head
will share His immortality.

C. S. LEWIS

When ten thousand times ten thousand times
ten thousand years have passed,
eternity will have just begun.

BILLY SUNDAY

I have written these things to you who believe
in the name of the Son of God, so that you
may know that you have eternal life.

1 JOHN 5:13 HCSB

EXAMPLE

You should be an example to the believers in speech,
in conduct, in love, in faith, in purity.

1 Timothy 4:12 HCSB

*Those who teach by their doctrine must teach
by their life, or else they pull down with one hand
what they build up with the other.*

Matthew Henry

*People are watching the way we act
more than they are listening to what we say.*

Max Lucado

*Be a good witness by the way you live. The way we
live is often more convincing than the words we say.*

Billy Graham

*Be such a man, and live such a life, that if every man
were such as you, and every life a life like yours,
this earth would be God's Paradise.*

Phillips Brooks

If we live in the Spirit, let us also walk in the Spirit.

Galatians 5:25 NKJV

EXCELLENCE

Do your work with enthusiasm.
Work as if you were serving the Lord,
not as if you were serving only men and women.

Ephesians 6:7 NCV

*The secret of living a life of excellence is merely
a matter of thinking thoughts of excellence.
Really, it's a matter of programming our minds
with the kind of information that will set us free.*

Charles Swindoll

*The quest for excellence is a mark of maturity.
The quest for power is childish.*

Max Lucado

*When love and skill work together,
expect a masterpiece.*

John Ruskin

Finally, brethren, whatever is true, whatever is honorable,
whatever is right, whatever is pure, whatever is lovely,
whatever is of good repute, if there is any excellence
and if anything worthy of praise, dwell on these things.

Ephesians 6:7 NCV

EXCUSES

So when you make a promise to God,
don't delay in following through,
for God takes no pleasure in fools.
Keep all the promises you make to him.

ECCLESIASTES 5:4 NLT

*Rationalization: It's what we do when we
substitute false explanations for true reasons.
It's when we cloud our actual motives
with nice-sounding excuses.*

CHARLES SWINDOLL

*Making up a string of excuses is
usually harder than doing the work.*

MARIE T. FREEMAN

*Make no excuses. Rationalize nothing.
Blame no one. Humble yourself.*

BETH MOORE

But prove yourselves doers of the word,
and not merely hearers who delude themselves.

JAMES 1:22 NASB

FAILURE

For though a righteous man
falls seven times, he rises again.

PROVERBS 24:16 NIV

Failure is one of life's most powerful teachers.
How we handle our failures determines whether
we're going to simply "get by" in life or "press on."

BETH MOORE

No amount of falls will really undo us
if we keep picking ourselves up after each one.

C. S. LEWIS

Be patient with everyone,
but above all with yourself.
I mean, do not be disturbed
because of your imperfections,
and always rise up bravely from a fall.

ST. FRANCIS DE SALES

If you listen to correction to improve your life,
you will live among the wise.

PROVERBS 15:31 NCV

FAITH

For truly I say to you, if you have faith
as a mustard seed, you shall say to this mountain,
"Move from here to there" and it shall move;
and nothing shall be impossible to you.

MATTHEW 17:20 NASB

Shout the shout of faith.
Nothing can withstand the triumphant faith
that links itself to omnipotence. The secret
of all successful living lies in this shout of faith.

HANNAH WHITALL SMITH

Faith does not concern itself with the entire journey.
One step is enough.

LETTIE COWMAN

I have learned that faith means trusting in advance
what will only make sense in reverse.

PHILLIP YANCEY

Blessed are they that have not seen,
and yet have believed.

JOHN 20:29 KJV

FAMILY

Choose for yourselves this day
whom you will serve ....
But as for me and my house,
we will serve the Lord.

Joshua 24:15 NKJV

*A family is a place where principles
are hammered out and honed
on the anvil of everyday living.*

Charles Swindoll

*I like to think of my family as a big,
beautiful patchwork quilt—each of us so different
yet stitched together by love and life experiences.*

Barbara Johnson

*The family circle is the
supreme conductor of Christianity.*

Henry Drummond

But if anyone does not provide for his own,
and especially for those of his household, he has
denied the faith and is worse than an unbeliever.

1 Timothy 5:8 NASB

FEAR

But He said to them, "It is I; do not be afraid."

JOHN 6:20 NKJV

*The presence of fear does not mean
you have no faith. Fear visits everyone.
But make your fear a visitor and not a resident.*

MAX LUCADO

*The Lord Jesus by His Holy Spirit is with me,
and the knowledge of His presence dispels
the darkness and allays any fears.*

BILL BRIGHT

*The presence of hope
in the invincible sovereignty
of God drives out fear.*

JOHN PIPER

The LORD is my light and my salvation—
whom should I fear?
The LORD is the stronghold of my life—
of whom should I be afraid?

PSALM 27:1 HCSB

FELLOWSHIP

Now I urge you, brothers, in the name of
our Lord Jesus Christ, that you all say the same thing,
that there be no divisions among you,
and that you be united with the same
understanding and the same conviction.

1 CORINTHIANS 1:10 HCSB

Be united with other Christians.
A wall with loose bricks is not good.
The bricks must be cemented together.

CORRIE TEN BOOM

Church-goers are like coals in a fire.
When they cling together, they keep the flame
aglow; when they separate, they die out.

BILLY GRAHAM

Our love to God is measured by our everyday
fellowship with others and the love it displays.

ANDREW MURRAY

Love one another fervently with a pure heart.

1 PETER 1:22 NKJV

FOCUS

Let us lay aside every weight, and the sin
which so easily ensnares us, and let us run
with endurance the race that is set before us.

HEBREWS 12:1 NKJV

*It seems essential, in relationships and all tasks,
that we concentrate only on
what is most significant and important.*

SØREN KIERKEGAARD

*As you organize your life, you must localize
and define it. You cannot do everything.*

PHILLIPS BROOKS

*Give me a person who says, "This one thing I do,"
and not "These fifty things I dabble in."*

D. L. MOODY

There is one thing I always do.
Forgetting the past and straining toward
what is ahead, I keep trying to reach the goal
and get the prize for which God called me . . . .

PHILIPPIANS 3:13–14 NCV

FOLLOWING CHRIST

"Follow Me," Jesus told them,
"and I will make you into fishers of men!"
Immediately they left their nets and followed Him.

MARK 1:17–18 HCSB

A disciple is a follower of Christ.
That means you take on His priorities as your own.
His agenda becomes your agenda.
His mission becomes your mission.

CHARLES STANLEY

The crucial question for each of us is this:
What do you think of Jesus, and do you yet
have a personal acquaintance with Him?

HANNAH WHITALL SMITH

This my song through endless ages:
Jesus led me all the way.

FANNY CROSBY

How happy is everyone who fears the LORD,
who walks in His ways!

PSALM 128:1 HCSB

FORGIVENESS

Judge not, and you shall not be judged.
Condemn not, and you shall not be condemned.
Forgive, and you will be forgiven.

LUKE 6:37 NKJV

Forgiveness is God's command.

MARTIN LUTHER

*Forgiveness is one of the most beautiful words
in the human vocabulary.
How much pain could be avoided
if we all learned the meaning of this word!*

BILLY GRAHAM

*He who cannot forgive others breaks
the bridge over which he himself must pass.*

CORRIE TEN BOOM

Above all, love each other deeply,
because love covers a multitude of sins.

1 PETER 4:8 NIV

FRIENDS AND FRIENDSHIP

A friend loves at all times,
and a brother is born for adversity.

PROVERBS 17:17 NIV

Friendship is one of the sweetest joys of life.
Many might have failed beneath the bitterness
of their trial had they not found a friend.

C. H. SPURGEON

Few delights can equal the presence
of one whom we trust utterly.

GEORGE MACDONALD

In friendship, God opens your eyes
to the glories of Himself.

JONI EARECKSON TADA

A friend is one who makes me do my best.

OSWALD CHAMBERS

As iron sharpens iron,
so people can improve each other.

PROVERBS 27:17 NCV

FUTURE

There is surely a future hope for you,
and your hope will not be cut off.

PROVERBS 23:18 NIV

Never be afraid to trust an
unknown future to a known God.

CORRIE TEN BOOM

It may be that the day of judgment will
dawn tomorrow; in that case, we shall gladly stop
working for a better future. But not before.

DIETRICH BONHOEFFER

Every experience God gives us, every person
He brings into our lives, is the perfect
preparation for the future that only He can see.

CORRIE TEN BOOM

For I know the thoughts that I think toward you,
says the Lord, thoughts of peace and not of evil,
to give you a future and a hope.
Then you will call upon Me and go and pray to Me,
and I will listen to you.

JEREMIAH 29:11–12 NKJV

GOD FIRST

But seek first the kingdom of God
and His righteousness, and all these things
will be provided for you.

Matthew 6:33 HCSB

*The most important thing you must decide
to do every day is put the Lord first.*

Elizabeth George

Christ is either Lord of all, or He is not Lord at all.

Hudson Taylor

*Jesus Christ is the first and last, author and finisher,
beginning and end, alpha and omega,
and by Him all other things hold together.
He must be first or nothing. God never comes next!*

Vance Havner

*When you live in the light of eternity,
your values change.*

Rick Warren

You shall have no other gods before Me.

Exodus 20:3 NKJV

GOD'S GUIDANCE

Trust in the LORD with all your heart, and lean
not on your own understanding; in all your ways
acknowledge Him, and He shall direct your paths.

PROVERBS 3:5–6 NKJV

When we are obedient,
God guides our steps and our stops.

CORRIE TEN BOOM

We have ample evidence that the Lord
is able to guide. The promises cover every
imaginable situation. All we need to do
is to take the hand He stretches out.

ELISABETH ELLIOT

I am satisfied that when the Almighty
wants me to do or not to do any particular thing,
He finds a way to let me know it.

ABRAHAM LINCOLN

The LORD says, "I will guide you along
the best pathway for your life.
I will advise you and watch over you."

PSALM 32:8 NLT

GOD'S PLAN

But as it is written: What no eye has seen
and no ear has heard, and what has never
come into a man's heart, is what
God has prepared for those who love Him.

1 CORINTHIANS 2:9 HCSB

God has no problems, only plans.
There is never panic in heaven.

CORRIE TEN BOOM

God's purpose is greater than our problems,
our pain and even our sin.

RICK WARREN

God has a course mapped out for your life,
and all the inadequacies in the world
will not change His mind.
He will be with you every step of the way.

CHARLES STANLEY

And yet, O LORD, you are our Father.
We are the clay, and you are the potter.
We are all formed by your hand.

ISAIAH 64:8 NLT

GOD'S PROMISES

Let us hold on to the confession of our hope without wavering, for He who promised is faithful.

HEBREWS 10:23 HCSB

The Bible is God's book of promises, and unlike the books of man, it does not change or go out of date.

BILLY GRAHAM

Beloved, God's promises can never fail to be accomplished, and those who patiently wait can never be disappointed, for a believing faith leads to realization.

LETTIE COWMAN

Don't let obstacles along the road to eternity shake your confidence in God's promises.

DAVID JEREMIAH

Let God's promises shine on your problems.

CORRIE TEN BOOM

As for God, his way is perfect: the word of the LORD is tried: he is a buckler to all those that trust in him.

PSALM 18:30 KJV

GOD'S SUPPORT

My grace is sufficient for you,
for my power is made perfect in weakness.

2 Corinthians 12:9 NIV

*The Lord God of heaven and earth,
the Almighty Creator, He who holds the universe
in His hand as though it were a very little thing,
He is your Shepherd, and He has charged Himself
with the care and keeping of you.*

Hannah Whitall Smith

*Put your hand into the hand of God.
He gives the calmness and serenity of heart and soul.*

Lettie Cowman

*The knowledge that we are never alone
calms the troubled sea of our lives
and speaks peace to our souls.*

A. W. Tozier

And my God will supply all your needs
according to His riches in glory in Christ Jesus.

Philippians 4:19 HCSB

GOD'S TIMING

Therefore humble yourselves under the mighty
hand of God, that He may exalt you in due time.

1 PETER 5:6 NKJV

*Teach us, O Lord, the disciplines of patience,
for to wait is often harder than to work.*

PETER MARSHALL

*We often hear about waiting on God,
which actually means that He is waiting
until we are ready. There is another side,
however. When we wait for God,
we are waiting until He is ready.*

LETTIE COWMAN

Will not the Lord's time be better than your time?

C. H. SPURGEON

He has made everything appropriate in its time.
He has also put eternity in their hearts,
but man cannot discover the work
God has done from beginning to end.

ECCLESIASTES 3:11 HCSB

GRATITUDE

Enter into His gates with thanksgiving, and into His courts with praise. Be thankful to Him, and bless His name. For the LORD is good; His mercy is everlasting, and His truth endures to all generations.

PSALM 100:4–5 NKJV

*God is in control, and therefore in everything
I can give thanks—not because of the situation
but because of the One who directs and rules over it.*

KAY ARTHUR

*If I succeed, I will give thanks.
If I fail, I will seek His grace.*

MAX LUCADO

*In the ordinary life, we hardly realize that we
receive a great deal more than we give, and that
it is only with gratitude that life becomes rich.*

DIETRICH BONHOEFFER

And whatever you do, in word or in deed,
do everything in the name of the Lord Jesus,
giving thanks to God the Father through Him.

COLOSSIANS 3:17 HCSB

HABITS

And so, dear brothers and sisters,
I plead with you to give your bodies to God.
Let them be a living and holy sacrifice—
the kind he will accept. When you think of what
he has done for you, is this too much to ask?

ROMANS 12:1 NLT

We first make our habits, then our habits make us.

JOHN DRYDEN

*Your little choices become habits that affect
the bigger decisions you make in life.*

ELIZABETH GEORGE

*Remember that your character
is the sum total of your habits.*

RICK WARREN

Who is wise and understanding among you?
He should show his works by good conduct
with wisdom's gentleness.

JAMES 3:13 HCSB

HAPPINESS

Those who listen to instruction will prosper;
those who trust the Lord will be happy.

Proverbs 16:20 NLT

Joy comes not from what we have but what we are.

C. H. Spurgeon

*Those who are the happiest
are not necessarily those for whom
life has been the easiest.
Emotional stability is an attitude.*

James Dobson

*When the dream of our heart is one that
God has planted there, a strange happiness flows
into us. At that moment, the spiritual resources
of the universe are released to help us.*

Catherine Marshall

If they obey and serve him,
they will spend the rest of their days in prosperity
and their years in contentment.

Job 36:11 NIV

HOPE

Let us hold fast the confession of our hope without wavering, for He who promised is faithful.

HEBREWS 10:23 NASB

The presence of hope in the invincible sovereignty of God drives out fear.

JOHN PIPER

Jesus gives us hope because He keeps us company, has a vision and knows the way we should go.

MAX LUCADO

The earth's troubles fade in the light of heaven's hope.

BILLY GRAHAM

If your hopes are being disappointed just now, it means that they are being purified.

OSWALD CHAMBERS

This hope we have as an anchor of the soul, a hope both sure and steadfast.

HEBREWS 6:19 NASB

HUMILITY

Always be humble, gentle, and patient,
accepting each other in love.

Ephesians 4:2 NCV

Pride builds walls between people,
humility builds bridges.

Rick Warren

God measures people by the small dimensions
of humility and not by the bigness of their
achievements or the size of their capabilities.

Billy Graham

The holy man is the most humble
man you can meet.

Oswald Chambers

Therefore humble yourselves under
the mighty hand of God, that He may
exalt you in due time, casting all
your care upon Him, for He cares for you.

1 Peter 5:6–7 NKJV

INTEGRITY

The one who lives with integrity lives securely,
but whoever perverts his ways will be found out.

PROVERBS 10:9 HCSB

*The single most important element
in any human relationship is honesty—
with oneself, with God, and with others.*

CATHERINE MARSHALL

*Integrity is keeping a commitment
even after circumstances have changed.*

DAVID JEREMIAH

*Integrity is the glue that holds
our way of life together.*

BILLY GRAHAM

*The commandment of absolute truthfulness is only
another name for the fullness of discipleship.*

DIETRICH BONHOEFFER

Good people will be guided by honesty;
dishonesty will destroy those who are not trustworthy.

PROVERBS 11:3 NCV

JESUS

The next day John saw Jesus coming toward him
and said, "Here is the Lamb of God,
who takes away the sin of the world!"

John 1:29 HCSB

*Trust God's Word and His power more than
you trust your own feelings and experiences.
Remember, your Rock is Christ, and it is the sea
that ebbs and flows with the tides, not Him.*

Lettie Cowman

*Ultimately, our relationship with Christ
is the one thing we cannot do without.*

Beth Moore

*The crucial question for each of us is this:
What do you think of Jesus, and do you yet
have a personal acquaintance with Him?*

Hannah Whitall Smith

Jesus Christ the same yesterday,
and today, and for ever.

Hebrews 13:8 KJV

JOY

Rejoice always, pray without ceasing,
in everything give thanks;
for this is the will of God in Christ Jesus for you.

1 Thessalonians 5:16–18 NKJV

Joy is the great note all throughout the Bible.

Oswald Chambers

*Joy comes not from what
we have but what we are.*

C. H. Spurgeon

Joy is the serious business of heaven.

C. S. Lewis

*Joy is the direct result of having God's
perspective on our daily lives
and the effect of loving our Lord enough
to obey His commands and trust His promises.*

Bill Bright

Rejoice in the Lord always.
Again I will say, rejoice!

Philippians 4:4 NKJV

JUDGING OTHERS

Judge not, and you shall not be judged.
Condemn not, and you shall not be condemned.
Forgive, and you will be forgiven.

LUKE 6:37 NKJV

*Don't judge other people more harshly
than you want God to judge you.*

MARIE T. FREEMAN

*Yes, let God be the Judge.
Your job today is to be a witness.*

WARREN WIERSBE

*We must learn to regard people less in the light
of what they do or omit to do,
and more in light of what they suffer.*

DIETRICH BONHOEFFER

Don't criticize one another, brothers.
He who criticizes a brother or judges his brother
criticizes the law and judges the law. But if you judge
the law, you are not a doer of the law but a judge.

JAMES 4:11 HCSB

LEADERSHIP

But a good leader plans to do good,
and those good things make him a good leader.

Isaiah 32:8 NCV

*A leader is one who knows the way,
goes the way, and shows the way.*

John Maxwell

*Servanthood does not nullify leadership;
it defines it.*

John Piper

*According to Scripture, virtually everything that truly
qualifies a person for leadership is directly related to
character. Integrity is the main issue that makes the
difference between a good leader and a bad one.*

John MacArthur

*Leaders become great, not because of their power,
but because of their ability to empower others.*

John Maxwell

Shepherd the flock of God which is among you.

1 Peter 5:2 NKJV

LIFE

I urge you to live a life worthy
of the calling you have received.

EPHESIANS 4:1 NIV

Jesus wants Life for us; Life with a capital L.

JOHN ELDREDGE

*The measure of a life, after all,
is not its duration but its donation.*

CORRIE TEN BOOM

You have life before you. Only you can live it.

HENRY DRUMMOND

*You can't control the length of your life—
but you can control its width and depth.*

JOHN MAXWELL

Jesus said to her, "I am the resurrection and the life.
The one who believes in Me, even if he dies, will live.
Everyone who lives and believes in Me
will never die—ever. Do you believe this?"

JOHN 11:25–26 HCSB

LOVE

And now abide faith, hope, love, these three;
but the greatest of these is love.

1 Corinthians 13:13 NKJV

Love always means sacrifice.

Elisabeth Elliot

*Line by line, moment by moment,
special times are etched into
our memories in the permanent ink
of everlasting love in our relationships.*

Gloria Gaither

Love does not dominate; it cultivates.

Johann Wolfgang von Goethe

Love is not getting, but giving.

Henry Van Dyke

A new commandment I give unto you,
that ye love one another; as I have loved you,
that ye also love one another.

John 13:34 KJV

MATERIALISM

Your life should be free from the love of money.
Be satisfied with what you have, for He Himself
has said, I will never leave you or forsake you.

HEBREWS 13:5 HCSB

*Where the soul is full of peace and joy,
outward surroundings and circumstances
are of comparatively little account.*

HANNAH WHITALL SMITH

*Contentment is possible
when we stop striving for more.*

CHARLES SWINDOLL

*I have held many things in my hands,
and have lost them all; but whatever I
have placed in God's hands, that I still possess.*

MARTIN LUTHER

No one can serve two masters.
For you will hate one and love the other,
or be devoted to one and despise the other.
You cannot serve both God and money.

LUKE 16:13 NLT

MIRACLES

No eye has seen, no ear has heard,
no mind has conceived what God
has prepared for those who love him.

1 CORINTHIANS 2:9 NIV

We honor God by asking for great things when
they are a part of His promise. We dishonor Him
and cheat ourselves when we ask for molehills
where He has promised mountains.

VANCE HAVNER

God's specialty is raising dead things to life
and making impossible things possible.
You don't have the need that exceeds His power.

BETH MOORE

Beware in your prayers, above everything else,
of limiting God, not only by unbelief,
but by fancying that you know what He can do.
Expect unexpected things.

ANDREW MURRAY

All things are possible for the one who believes.

MARK 9:23 NCV

MODERATION

Moderation is better than muscle,
self-control better than political power.

Proverbs 16:32 MSG

*Virtue, even attempted virtue,
brings light; indulgence brings fog.*

C. S. Lewis

*If your desires be endless,
your cares and fears will be so, too.*

Thomas Fuller

Riches enlarge, rather than satisfy appetites.

Thomas Fuller

The first lesson in Christ's school is self-denial.

Matthew Henry

I discipline my body and bring it under
strict control, so that after preaching to others,
I myself will not be disqualified.

1 Corinthians 9:27 HCSB

OBEDIENCE

We must obey God rather than men.

ACTS 5:29 NASB

God has laid down spiritual laws which,
if obeyed, bring harmony and fulfillment,
but, if disobeyed, bring discord and disorder.

BILLY GRAHAM

The golden rule for understanding in spiritual matters
is not intellect, but obedience.

OSWALD CHAMBERS

Obedience is the key to every door.

GEORGE MACDONALD

When we are obedient,
God guides our steps and our stops.

CORRIE TEN BOOM

Now by this we know that we know Him,
if we keep His commandments.

1 JOHN 2:3 NKJV

OPPORTUNITIES

But as it is written: What no eye has seen
and no ear has heard, and what has never
come into a man's heart, is what God
has prepared for those who love Him.

1 Corinthians 2:9 HCSB

*We are all faced with a series of
great opportunities brilliantly disguised
as impossible situations.*

Charles Swindoll

*If all things are possible with God, then all things
are possible to him who believes in Him.*

Corrie ten Boom

*When God closes one door,
He often opens another—if we seek it.*

Billy Graham

Remember ye not the former things,
neither consider the things of old.
Behold, I will do a new thing.

Isaiah 43:18–19 KJV

OPTIMISM

The LORD is my light and my salvation—
whom should I fear? The LORD is the stronghold
of my life—of whom should I be afraid?

PSALM 27:1 HCSB

*Two types of voices command your
attention today. Negative ones fill your
mind with doubt, bitterness, and fear.
Positive ones purvey hope and strength.
Which one will you choose to heed?*

MAX LUCADO

*Never yield to gloomy anticipation.
Place your hope and confidence in God.
He has no record of failure.*

LETTIE COWMAN

*All things work together for good.
Fret not, nor fear!*

LETTIE COWMAN

But if we look forward to something we don't
have yet, we must wait patiently and confidently.

ROMANS 8:25 NLT

PAST

One thing I do, forgetting those things
which are behind and reaching forward
to those things which are ahead, I press
toward the goal for the prize of
the upward call of God in Christ Jesus.

PHILIPPIANS 3:13–14 NKJV

*Our past experiences may have
made us the way we are,
but we don't have to stay that way.*

JOYCE MEYER

*Trust the past to God's mercy, the present to God's
love, and the future to God's providence.*

ST. AUGUSTINE

*Don't be bound by the past and its failures.
But don't forgets its lessons either.*

BILLY GRAHAM

Do not remember the former things, nor consider
the things of old. Behold, I will do a new thing.

ISAIAH 43:18–19 NKJV

PATIENCE

Patience of spirit is better than
haughtiness of spirit.

ECCLESIASTES 7:8 NASB

*Teach us, O Lord, the disciplines of patience,
for to wait is often harder than to work.*

PETER MARSHALL

Patience is the companion of wisdom.

ST. AUGUSTINE

*Patience graciously, compassionately,
and with understanding, judges the faults
of others without unjust criticism.*

BILLY GRAHAM

*Some of your greatest blessings
come with patience.*

WARREN WIERSBE

A man's wisdom gives him patience;
it is to his glory to overlook an offense.

PROVERBS 19:11 NIV

PERFECTIONISM

If you wait for perfect conditions,
you will never get anything done.

*He who waits until circumstances
completely favor his undertaking
will never accomplish anything.*

MARTIN LUTHER

*Better to do something imperfectly
than to do nothing flawlessly.*

ROBERT SCHULLER

*Strive for excellence, not perfection,
because we don't live in a perfect world.*

JOYCE MEYER

One thing I do, forgetting those things
which are behind and reaching forward
to those things which are ahead,
I press toward the goal for the prize
of the upward call of God in Christ Jesus.

PHILIPPIANS 3:13–14 NKJV

PERSEVERANCE

Let us not become weary in doing good,
for at the proper time we will reap
a harvest if we do not give up.

GALATIANS 6:9 NIV

*Everyone gets discouraged. The question is:
Are you going to give up or get up? It's a choice.*

JOHN MAXWELL

*Patience and diligence,
like faith, remove mountains.*

WILLIAM PENN

*Success or failure can be pretty well predicted
by the degree to which the heart is fully in it.*

JOHN ELDREDGE

*No amount of falls will really undo us
if we keep picking ourselves up after each one.*

C. S. LEWIS

Finishing is better than starting.
Patience is better than pride.

ECCLESIASTES 7:8 NLT

PLANNING

But a noble person plans noble things;
he stands up for noble causes.

ISAIAH 32:8 HCSB

*It is important to set goals because
if you do not have a plan, a goal, a direction,
a purpose, and a focus, you are not going
to accomplish anything for the glory of God.*

BILL BRIGHT

*Make no little plans. They have no magic
to stir men's blood. Make big plans: Aim high
in hope and work, remembering that a noble,
logical diagram once recorded will not die.*

DANIEL HUDSON BURNHAM

*Let our advance worrying become
advance thinking and planning.*

WINSTON CHURCHILL

The wise see danger ahead and avoid it,
but fools keep going and get into trouble.

PROVERBS 22:3 NCV

PRAYER

Rejoice always, pray without ceasing,
in everything give thanks; for this is the will
of God in Christ Jesus for you.

1 Thessalonians 5:16-18 NKJV

Don't pray when you feel like it.
Have an appointment with the Lord and keep it.

Corrie ten Boom

It is impossible to overstate the need
for prayer in the fabric of family life.

James Dobson

Any concern that is too small
to be turned into a prayer is
too small to be made into a burden.

Corrie ten Boom

No man is greater than his prayer life.

Leonard Ravenhill

Is anyone among you suffering? He should pray.

James 5:13 HCSB

PRIDE

God resists the proud,
but gives grace to the humble.

JAMES 4:6 HCSB

*It is very easy to overestimate the importance
of our own achievements in comparison
with what we owe others.*

DIETRICH BONHOEFFER

*Pride builds walls between people,
humility builds bridges.*

RICK WARREN

*The world's smallest package
is a man wrapped up in himself.*

CHARLES SWINDOLL

All pride is idolatry.

JOHN WESLEY

God resists the proud,
but gives grace to the humble.

JAMES 4:6 HCSB

220

PROCRASTINATION

When you make a vow to God,
do not delay in fulfilling it.
He has no pleasure in fools;
fulfill your vow.

ECCLESIASTES 5:4 NIV

*Our grand business is, not to see
what lies dimly at a distance,
but to do what lies closely at hand.*

THOMAS CARLYLE

*Now is the only time worth having,
because indeed it is the only time we have.*

C. H. SPURGEON

*Every duty which we omit obscures some
truth which we should have known.*

JOHN RUSKIN

Whenever we have the opportunity,
we should do good to everyone,
especially to our Christian brothers and sisters.

GALATIANS 6:10 NLT

PURPOSE

In Him we were also made His inheritance,
predestined according to the purpose
of the One who works out everything in
agreement with the decision of His will.

EPHESIANS 1:11 HCSB

*The easiest way to discover the purpose of
an invention is to ask the creator of it. The same
is true for discovering your life's purpose: Ask God.*

RICK WARREN

*There's some task which the God
of all the universe, the great Creator,
has for you to do, and which will
remain undone and incomplete,
until by faith and obedience,
you step into the will of God.*

ALAN REDPATH

We must do the works of Him
who sent Me while it is day.
Night is coming when no one can work.

JOHN 9:4 HCSB

QUIET TIME

Be still, and know that I am God.

Psalm 46:10 KJV

Strength is found not in busyness
and noise but in quietness.

LETTIE COWMAN

Nothing in all creation
is so like God as stillness.

GOETHE

The world is full of noise.
Might we not set ourselves
to learn silence, stillness, solitude?

ELISABETH ELLIOT

God's voice is still and quiet
and easily buried under
an avalanche of clamor.

CHARLES STANLEY

Listen in silence before me.

ISAIAH 41:1 NLT

REST

Come unto me, all ye that labor and are
heavy laden, and I will give you rest.

MATTHEW 11:28 KJV

*Prescription for a happier and healthier life:
resolve to slow your pace; learn to say
no gracefully; reject the temptation
to chase after more pleasures, more hobbies,
and more social entanglements.*

JAMES DOBSON

*Life is strenuous. See that your clock
does not run down.*

LETTIE COWMAN

*Go to bed. Whatever you are
staying up for isn't worth it.*

ANDY ROONEY

Take My yoke upon you and learn from Me,
because I am gentle and humble in heart,
and you will find rest for your souls.
For My yoke is easy and My burden is light.

MATTHEW 11:29–30 HCSB

SIMPLICITY

Better a little with the fear of the LORD
than great treasure with turmoil.

PROVERBS 15:16 HCSB

*The characteristic of the life of a saint
is essentially elemental simplicity.*

OSWALD CHAMBERS

*The more complicated life becomes, the more
we need to quiet our souls before God.*

ELISABETH ELLIOT

*Out of the freedom from worry that
God's generosity provides comes an impulse
toward simplicity rather than accumulation.*

JOHN PIPER

*Nobody is going to simplify your life for you.
You've got to simplify things for yourself.*

MARIE T. FREEMAN

The LORD preserves the simple;
I was brought low, and He saved me.

PSALM 116:6 NAS

SPIRITUAL GROWTH

I remind you to fan into flames
the spiritual gift God gave you.

2 TIMOTHY 1:6 NLT

Grow, dear friends, but grow, I beseech you,
in God's way, which is the only true way.

HANNAH WHITALL SMITH

God's ultimate goal for your life on earth
is not comfort, but character development.
He wants you to grow up spiritually
and become like Christ.

RICK WARREN

Measure your growth in grace
by your sensitivity to sin.

OSWALD CHAMBERS

But grow in the grace and knowledge
of our Lord and Savior Jesus Christ. To Him
be the glory both now and forever. Amen.

2 PETER 3:18 NKJV

STRENGTH

He gives strength to the weary, and to him
who lacks might He increases power.

ISAIAH 40:29 NASB

The strength that we claim from God's Word
does not depend on circumstances.
Circumstances will be difficult,
but our strength will be sufficient.

CORRIE TEN BOOM

God is in control. He may not take away
trials or make detours for us,
but He strengthens us through them.

BILLY GRAHAM

The truth is, God's strength is fully revealed
when our strength is depleted.

LIZ CURTIS HIGGS

Have faith in the LORD your God,
and you will stand strong. Have faith
in his prophets, and you will succeed.

2 CHRONICLES 20:20 NCV

STRESS

Peace I leave with you; My peace I give to you;
not as the world gives do I give to you. Do not let
your heart be troubled, nor let it be fearful.

JOHN 14:27 NASB

*In times of stress, the best thing we can do
for each other is to listen with our ears and
our hearts and to be assured that our questions
are just as important as our answers.*

FRED ROGERS

*A day of worry is more exhausting
than a week of work.*

JOHN LUBBOCK

*Quiet minds cannot be perplexed
or frightened, but go on in fortune
or misfortune at their own private pace,
like a clock during a thunderstorm.*

ROBERT LOUIS STEVENSON

I find rest in God; only he gives me hope.

PSALM 62:5 NCV

TALENTS AND ABILITIES

Now there are diversities of gifts,
but the same Spirit.

1 CORINTHIANS 12:4 KJV

*Our purpose should be to discover the gifts He
has given us and to use those gifts faithfully
and joyfully in His service, without either envying
or disparaging the gifts we do not have.*

JOHN MACARTHUR

*You weren't an accident. You weren't mass
produced. You aren't an assembly-line product.
You were deliberately planned, specifically
gifted, and lovingly positioned on the Earth
by the Master Craftsman.*

MAX LUCADO

*If others don't use their gifts,
you get cheated, and if you don't use
your gifts, they get cheated.*

RICK WARREN

Do not neglect the gift that is in you.

1 TIMOTHY 4:14 NKJV

TEMPTATION

Be sober, be vigilant; because your adversary
the devil walks about like a roaring lion,
seeking whom he may devour.

1 PETER 5:8 NKJV

*The first step on the way to victory
is to recognize the enemy.*

CORRIE TEN BOOM

*It is not the temptations you have,
but the decision you make
about them, that counts.*

BILLY GRAHAM

*If your mind is filled with the Word of God,
then it can't be filled with impure thoughts.*

DAVID JEREMIAH

Watch therefore, and pray always that
you may be counted worthy to escape
all these things that will come to pass,
and to stand before the Son of Man.

LUKE 21:36 NKJV

THOUGHTS

Be careful what you think,
because your thoughts run your life.

PROVERBS 4:23 NCV

*The things we think are the things that feed
our souls. If we think on pure and lovely things,
we shall grow pure and lovely like them;
and the converse is equally true.*

HANNAH WHITALL SMITH

*When you think on the powerful truths
of Scripture, God uses His Word
to change your way of thinking.*

ELIZABETH GEORGE

*Your life today is a result of your thinking
yesterday. Your life tomorrow will be
determined by what you think today.*

JOHN MAXWELL

Set your mind on things above,
not on things on the earth.

COLOSSIANS 3:2 NKJV

TIME MANAGEMENT

Teach us to number our days carefully
so that we may develop wisdom in our hearts.

Psalm 90:12 HCSB

*Do you love life? Then do not squander time,
for that's the stuff life is made of.*

Ben Franklin

*Time is the coin of your life. It is the only coin
you have, and only you can determine
how it will be spent. Be careful lest
you let other people spend it for you.*

Carl Sandburg

*The greatest waste in all the earth
is our waste of the time
God has given us each day.*

Billy Graham

To everything there is a season,
a time for every purpose under heaven.

Ecclesiastes 3:1 NKJV

TODAY

This is the day the Lord has made.
We will rejoice and be glad in it.

Psalm 118:24 NLT

Today is mine. Tomorrow is none of my business.
If I peer anxiously into the fog of the future,
I will strain my spiritual eyes so that I will not
see clearly what is required of me now.

Elisabeth Elliot

Yesterday is the tomb of time, and tomorrow
is the womb of time. Only now is yours.

R. G. Lee

The present is the only time in which
any duty may be done or grace received.

C. S. Lewis

The one word in the spiritual vocabulary is now.

Oswald Chambers

Rejoice in the Lord always.
I will say it again: Rejoice!

Philippians 4:4 HCSB

TRUSTING GOD

Trust in the L
ORD with all your heart, and lean not
on your own understanding; in all your ways
acknowledge Him, and He shall direct your paths.

P
ROVERBS 3:5–6 NKJV

*One of the marks of spiritual maturity is
the quiet confidence that God is in control,
without the need to understand
why He does what He does.*

C
HARLES SWINDOLL

*Faith and obedience are bound up
in the same bundle. He that obeys God, trusts God;
and he that trusts God, obeys God.*

C. H. S
PURGEON

*Never be afraid to trust an unknown
future to a known God.*

C
ORRIE TEN BOOM

The fear of man is a snare, but the one
who trusts in the L
ORD is protected.

P
ROVERBS 29:25 HCSB

VALUES

Do not conform any longer to the pattern
of this world, but be transformed by the
renewing of your mind. Then you will be able
to test and approve what God's will is—
his good, pleasing and perfect will.

ROMANS 12:2 NIV

The Reference Point for the Christian is the Bible.
All values, judgments, and attitudes must be
gauged in relationship to this Reference Point.

RUTH BELL GRAHAM

We glorify God by living lives that honor Him.

BILLY GRAHAM

Eternal values, not temporal ones,
should become the deciding factors
for your decisions.

RICK WARREN

So I strive always to keep my conscience
clear before God and man.

ACTS 24:16 NIV

WISDOM AND UNDERSTANDING

If you need wisdom—if you want to know
what God wants you to do—ask him, and he
will gladly tell you. He will not resent your asking.

JAMES 1:5 NLT

Wisdom is the right use of knowledge.
To know is not to be wise. There is no fool
so great as the knowing fool. But, to know
how to use knowledge is to have wisdom.

C. H. SPURGEON

Wisdom is the power to see and the inclination
to choose the best and highest goal,
together with the surest means of attaining it.

J. I. PACKER

Wisdom is doing now what you are
going to be happy with later on.

JOYCE MEYER

The fear of the LORD is the beginning of knowledge,
but fools despise wisdom and instruction.

PROVERBS 1:7 NKJV

HARD WORK AND DEDICATION

Whatever you do, do it enthusiastically,
as something done for the Lord and not for men.

COLOSSIANS 3:23 HCSB

*Work is a blessing. God has so arranged the world
that work is necessary, and He gives us hands
and strength to do it. The enjoyment of leisure
would be nothing if we had only leisure.*

ELISABETH ELLIOT

*It is our best work that God wants,
not the dregs of our exhaustion.
I think He must prefer quality to quantity.*

GEORGE MACDONALD

*What is needed for happy effectual
service is simply to put your work
into the Lord's hand, and leave it there.*

HANNAH WHITALL SMITH

We must do the works of Him who sent Me while
it is day. Night is coming when no one can work.

JOHN 9:4 HCSB

WORSHIP

I was glad when they said unto me,
Let us go into the house of the LORD.

PSALM 122:1 KJV

*Worship in the truest sense takes place only
when our full attention is on God—His glory,
majesty, love, and compassion.*

BILLY GRAHAM

*We must worship in truth. Worship is not just
an emotional exercise but a response
of the heart built on truth about God.*

ERWIN LUTZER

*Worship is an inward reverence, the bowing down
of the soul in the presence of God.*

ELIZABETH GEORGE

Happy are those who hear the joyful call
to worship, for they will walk in the light
of your presence, LORD.

PSALM 89:15 NLT

A FINAL NOTE TO READERS

I am come that they might have life, and that they
might have it more abundantly.

John 10:10 KJV

There are, of course, many components to a well-lived life. But throughout this text, we've attempted to convey the core principles that we believe will help you achieve The Good Life that Jesus describes in John 10:10.

God has a plan for everything, including you. As a part of that plan, He intends that you experience abundance and joy in this life and perfect joy throughout all eternity. But perhaps your vision of what God intends for your life is not quite as clear as you would like. If so, we pray that the ideas in this book have been helpful.

If you sincerely seek God's guidance for your life, He will give it. But, He will make His revelations known to you in a way—and at a time—of His choosing, not yours. So, if you're sincerely seeking to know God's will for your life, don't be worried if you haven't yet received a "final" answer. The final answer, of course, will come not in this world, but in the next.

If you've encountered circumstances that you don't fully understand, don't be discouraged. Instead of fretting about the future, open your heart to God in the present moment. Listen to Him, and do the work that He has placed before you. Then, rest assured that if you genuinely trust God and accept the salvation of His only begotten Son, God's plans for you will be as perfect as His love.

Blessings from Our Family to Yours,
Ken and Karen Gonyer

ABOUT THE AUTHORS

Karen Gonyer is a writer, teacher, and financial coach. She enjoys quilting, reading, and spending time with family. Ken Gonyer recently received a diploma in Advanced Biblical Studies from Liberty University and enjoys writing, preaching, and spending time in nature. Karen and Ken are the authors of *How Do I Stop Stressing About Money* (Smith Freeman Publishing, 2018), a practical guide to managing money and reducing stress. They live in the beautiful Shenandoah Valley of Virginia.